WEAPONS AND EQUIPMENT
OF THE VICTORIAN SOLDIER

WEAPONS AND EQUIPMENT
OF THE
VICTORIAN SOLDIER

DONALD FEATHERSTONE
Illustrated by John Mollo

BLANDFORD PRESS
POOLE
DORSET

Blandford Press Ltd,
Link House, West Street,
Poole, Dorset BH15 1LL

First published 1978
Copyright © 1978 Donald Featherstone
ISBN 0 7137 0847 6

Printed in Great Britain by
Fletcher & Son Ltd, Norwich

CONTENTS

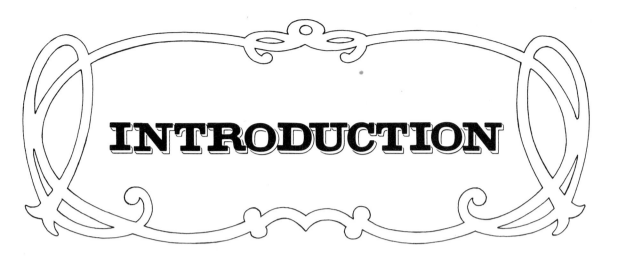

INTRODUCTION

The Victorian period was an age of great change and there were advances in practically every field, nevertheless the British Army altered so little that the line infantryman who fought at Waterloo in 1815 could have efficiently taken his place in the ranks at Omdurman in 1898! Fettered for half a century by the last major victory at Waterloo and the stern dictates of the conqueror Wellington, the British Army seemed unable to accept changes other than those which arose from the glorious traditions of the past. The Duke, readily supported by Adjutants-General Sir John MacDonald and Sir George Brown, ignored the progressive advance of Continental nations in the science of war; at the same time he was firmly convinced that artillery was an inferior weapon to the musket. He had won battles with the old smooth-bore Brown Bess, heavy accoutrements, uncomfortable chokers, suffocating stocks and restricting ill-slung knapsacks and it was his inflexible maxim that what had been accomplished before could be achieved again with the same instruments.

Also, he believed that if the Army became too costly the Nation would resent them, so the Duke kept his soldiers hidden in squalid overcrowded back-street barracks, and doggedly opposed increases in their pay. He was backed by a succession of governments that believed more money would make the soldier increasingly licentious and drunken, necessitating greater severity of discipline. At the outbreak of the Crimean War, the soldier received a minimum of a shilling a day plus a penny per day beer money, less $4\frac{1}{2}d$. deducted for cost of rations; from the remaining $8\frac{1}{2}d$. per day was subtracted Regimental stoppages and the cost of the soldier's 'necessaries', such as cleaning materials. In 1873, the free daily ration of food raised the soldier's rate of pay to one shilling a day, but his beer money was abolished; it was not until 1898 that the private soldier was assured of a full shilling a day.

Although conditions were well known to be bad, Victorian men 'took on' to be a soldier through stark necessity – Jack Frost was the best recruiting sergeant. During the potato famines in Ireland, young Irishmen despairingly discovered the British Army to be their only means of obtaining food, clothing and a roof over their heads; Regimental rolls began to resemble Irish parish registers and the onward march of the British Empire was milestoned by graves bearing Irish names. The Army had become an asylum for the scourings of the Nation with magistrates giving prisoners the choice of prison, transportation or becoming soldiers. Having taken the Queen's shilling, the recruit, often of poor physique and low health standards, was subjected to a process of 'breaking', tamed and cowed into submission by savage drilling and remorseless bullying which, together with unhealthy living conditions, gave the Army a death-rate many times higher than that of the civilian population. For much of the Victorian era, the soldier

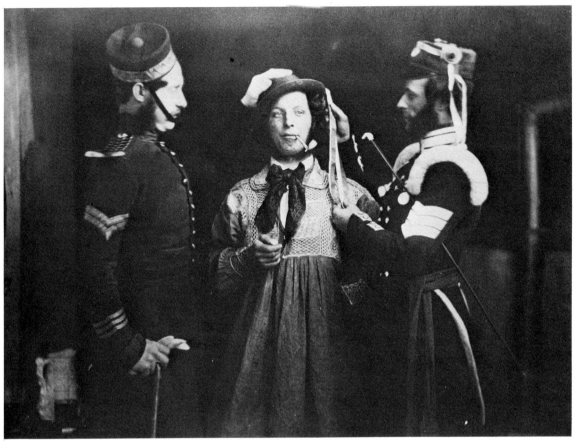

Fig. 1. Recruiting sergeants (Left: Heavy Cavalry; right: Infantry), congratulating a well set-up recruit, c. 1854. A reconstructed scene from the collection of photographs of 'Crimean Heroes'.

was an object of derision in an unpopular calling, despised by the public he served as the scum of the earth.

If the soldier failed in his duties through fear, ignorance, stupidity or bloody-mindedness, the common punishment was pack-drill imposed so ferociously and for so long as to reduce the victim to a state of complete exhaustion. Through pressure of public indignation slaves were emancipated at the time of Victoria's accession in 1837, but it was still permissible to flog a British soldier in 1881. Then the Army Discipline Act abolished flogging, replacing it on active service with Field Punishment Number 1 involving lashing men to a gun-wheel for a specified number of hours.

In the Crimea in 1854, 39 years after Waterloo, the Army commanded by officers who had fought in the Peninsular War, was composed of hardened soldiers of the old

school – prematurely aged and undermined by drink, appalling living conditions and ferocious discipline – stolid, shrewd, hard-swearing, illiterate, long-suffering men. It took the unsparing efforts of two reforming spirits – Secretary-at-War Sydney Herbert and Florence Nightingale – to change this old order and introduce a milder atmosphere into the life of the Army so that the long-service soldier faded from the scene along with many old and repressive ideas.

The 'barrack-square bound' Victorian soldier spent much of his service life in and around grim and grimy buildings in the heart of crowded cities, or garrisoning ancient forts and castles; outdoor training rarely took place because it interfered with farming and the grazing rights of common-land. The slow poison of Home Service with its stifling routine and suppression of initiative could have drugged the soldier into

Fig. 2. A recruiting sergeant leading a party of recruits for the Crimea through the streets of London. (An engraving from L'Illustration.)

Fig. 3. Below: 'The Recruiter.' A permanent staff recruiting sergeant handing the 'Queen's shilling' to a recruit. (From the photograph album of Sergeant Lawson, 35th Foot, 1865–70.)

inertia, but it never seemed to affect his undoubted character and constitutional courage, nor quell his burning desire for active service. Providentially, on the North-West Frontier of India belligerent, brave and tactically-brilliant tribesmen obligingly supplied the Victorian soldier with practical experience of active service conditions. As the century ran its course, the soldier spent less and less time in Britain, his entitlement to five years at home for every ten years overseas could only be fulfilled by steadily reducing overseas garrisons, so that any threatening situation in India or Africa cut into already curtailed periods of home service. To these lengthy periods overseas must be added the months spent at sea on passage to and from remote parts of the Empire when, in those early days of steam, both the perils of the sea and generally atrocious conditions had to be endured on troopships.

During the 64 years of Queen Victoria's reign the British soldier took part in more

Fig. 4. Recruiting sergeants outside a public-house in Westminster, 1875. Left to right: *6th or Inniskilling Dragoons; 14th the King's Hussars; Royal Engineers; Royal Scots Greys; 5th Dragoon Guards; 6th Dragoon Guards.*

than sixty military campaigns involving at least 400 separate battles. Fighting in all five continents of the world, there was hardly a year in this long and nostalgically glorious period when the British Army was not occupied in some far-flung corner of the world. It is an impressive roster:

1837 – Canada.
1838 – Aden; Afghanistan; Persia.
1840 – China; the Levant.
1841 – Afghanistan.
1843 – Gwalior; Scinde.
1845–6 – Punjab.
1846 – New Zealand; South Africa.
1847 – South Africa.
1848 – North-West Frontier of India; South Africa.
1849 – North-West Frontier of India; Punjab.
1850 – North-West Frontier of India.
1851 – South Africa.
1852 – Burma; North-West Frontier of India; South Africa.
1853 – North-West Frontier of India.
1854 – Australia; North-West Frontier of India; Russia (Crimea).
1855 – Russia.
1856 – Persia.
1857 – Bengal; Central India; China; Oudh.
1858 – Bengal; Central India; North-West Frontier of India; Oudh.
1859 – Bengal; China; Oudh.
1860 – China.
1861 – New Zealand; Sikkim.
1863 – Ambela; New Zealand.
1864 – Bhutan; North-West Frontier of India; Japan; New Zealand.
1866 – North-West Frontier of India.
1867 – North-West Frontier of India.
1868 – Abyssinia.
1870 – Canada.
1871 – Lushai.
1873 – Ashanti.
1874 – Ashanti.
1875 – Malay.
1877 – North-West Frontier of India; South Africa.
1878 – Afghanistan; North-West Frontier of India; Malta.
1879 – Afghanistan; North-West Frontier of India; Natal.

1880 – North-West Frontier of India.
1881 – North-West Frontier of India; Transvaal.
1882 – Egypt.
1883 – Egypt.
1884 – Burma; Egypt; North-West Frontier of India; Sudan.
1885 – Burma; Sudan.
1886 – Burma.
1887 – West Africa.
1888 – North-West Frontier of India; Sikkim; Tibet.
1890 – North-West Frontier of India; Somaliland.
1891 – Hunza; North-West Frontier of India; Manipur.
1892 – Chilas; North-West Frontier of India; West Africa.
1893 – West Africa.
1894 – Chitral; Waziristan; West Africa.
1895 – Chitral.
1896 – Egypt; Mashonaland; Mombasa; Sudan; Zanzibar.
1897 – Benin; North-West Frontier of India; Sudan.
1898 – Buner; Egypt; Sudan; Jubaland; Niger; South Africa; Transvaal.
1899 – South Africa; Transvaal.
1900 – Ashanti; China; South Africa; Transvaal.
1901 – South Africa; Transvaal.

Each of these campaigns was typical yet unique, their most remarkable feature being the men who fought them – the common soldier, the man in the ranks – Kipling's immortal Ortheris, Mulvaney and Learoyd serve as typical representatives of them all. Obeying orders and doing their duty under the most arduous conditions, lacking knowledge of cause or reason, the British Regular soldiers carried out punitive expeditions on the Indian Frontier, avenged wrongs in Abyssinia, Afghanistan and India, engaged in political wars of expediency against Zulus and Egyptians. Throughout the entire Victorian era, the British soldier fought and died amid inhospitable alien terrain where the difference between outright success and stalemate was annihilation. Drilled into blind obedience by harsh discipline, he displayed courage, endurance and humour

Fig. 5. A private of an infantry regiment standing by his kit layout, c. 1880. The folding bed and general barrack-room layout were still to be seen in the 1940s.

under appalling conditions to defeat superior numbers of such natural warriors as Sikhs, Maoris, Zulus, Pathans and Dervishes. His successes cannot be entirely credited to the Martini–Henry rifle and the mountain gun, much was owed to the constant emphasis on Regimental honour, tradition, comradeship and spirit which together with high standards of duty, produced first-class soldiers.

His opponents stoutly played their part, rarely displaying cowardice or ignoble qualities and on repeated occasions revealing incredible courage and dignity in spite of invariably taking casualties at least ten times as high as those they inflicted upon the British. The natural barbarity and savagery of these native warriors was countered by those occasions when British soldiers displayed brutality, prejudice and ruthlessness. Sikhs, Maoris and Dervishes earned the respect of

their Regular opponents; the Matabele, the Chinese, the Afghans and the Egyptians all fought in totally different fashions and displayed varying qualities of discipline but were none the less formidable on that account. The bravery and recklessness shown by the Sudanese in the early 1880s and against Kitchener in 1898 forced the Regulars to return to old orders of battle and fight in tactical square formation, and there was a marked resemblance between the tactics of Omdurman in 1898 and Waterloo in 1815.

All manner of opponents were encountered with little prior knowledge of their strength, weapons, fighting abilities or methods of warfare – except that none of them fought in the same fashion. In the three-year period 1878–81 and in one single quarter of the African Continent, British troops came successively into conflict with

6

Fig. 6. Hamilton Cavalry Barracks, 1873. (From an album of photographs belonging to the Royal Dragoons.)

Fig. 7. The half-yearly inspection of the Royal Engineers in progress in front of the depot at Chatham, 1856. The rear ranks have turned about and all have their kits laid out on the ground in front of them.

Fig. 8. H.M. Troopship Orontes *in Table Bay, c. 1881.*

the astonishingly different methods of combat respectively employed by Kaffirs, Zulus and Boers; simultaneously the Regular Army were also heavily committed on the North-West Frontier of India and in Afghanistan. If unforeseen, the fresh features of each war invariably resulted in difficulties and even grievous misfortune to the Regulars – the massacre at Isandhlwana, one of the worst disasters to befall British troops in Queen Victoria's reign occurred because of a total misconception of the enemy's tactics plus a lack of screwdrivers to open ammunition boxes so that the British force ran out of bullets.

Nature, rather than hostile armies, was the main enemy as climate and conditions affected the health of the British Regulars so that more casualties were due to sickness than to fire and sword. These primitive conditions allied to the enemy's style of fighting and the singular features of the theatre-of-war caused the conduct of Victorian wars to widely diverge from the conditions and principles of regular warfare of the period, where each side was well aware of what to expect from the enemy and both adversaries were

governed by specific common rules. These 'small wars' against savages and semi-civilized races saw small expeditions, often unsuitably equipped, marching out to take on superior numbers of warrior-races fighting on their own terrain. Wearing red coats in the early years and then in khaki, British and native infantry, cavalry and artillery marched in columns that slithered slowly through the dust like a crimson caterpillar as elephants, camels and bullocks plodded along with donkeys and yaks, with clattering and jingling mules carrying the little mountain guns.

The strength of these forces of civilization was also their weakness as the arms and equipment that brought tactical superiority and eventual success also burdened them with non-combatant services and tied them to their base and to lines of communications. Organized Regular forces, backed by all the resources of science, wealth, manpower and navies, were at an undoubted strategical disadvantage in these small wars.

Not all the enemy were savage or irregular warriors; some battles were fought against an enemy trained and organized like regular

Fig. 9. 'Eight 'undred fighting Englishmen, the Colonel, and the band.' An infantry battalion takes to the road during the Secunderabad Camp of Exercise, December 1892.

Fig. 10. 'Home again.' Crimean veterans disembarking, 1856. (From the engraving by W. T. Davey after H. O'Neill, A.R.A.)

troops by instructors with knowledge and experience of European methods; so that subsequent operations resembled the regular warfare of the day. This occurred in the Punjab in 1845–6 and 1849 when, after some of the fiercest fought engagements in Colonial history, the British Regiments of the Honourable East India Company (inauspiciously supported by native troops) defeated the martial Sikhs. During the Indian Mutiny of 1857, the British Regulars and those native units who remained loyal were faced by field armies of much greater strength, composed of experienced and competent Sepoys trained along British lines. In 1879, Cetewayo's Zulus were a well-organized and disciplined army capable of carrying out battlefield manoeuvres with order and precision, efficiently employing primitive but effective weapons.

9

Fig. 11. Troops assembling on the deck of a troopship, c. 1880.

In the Crimea the British and their French allies faced a trained and well-armed European army, fortunately commanded by generals even more inefficient than those of the Allies – otherwise the tactics and the harsh climate could have resulted in a major disaster to British arms. The only other white opponents faced by the British during the whole of the Victorian era were the Boers in 1881 and 1898–1902. Commanded by born leaders, the daring and well-armed Boers, gifted with unusual mobility and exceptional cunning, were a highly formidable enemy on their own familiar terrain. The costly lessons learned in defeating them greatly affected the training of the British Army during the decade that followed.

For the first 40 years of Victoria's reign, her army proceeded overseas and went into action in full dress uniform – tight scarlet tunics with high leather stock, trousers tightly strapped over Wellington boots and a shako that gave no protection from the tropical sun. The gorgeous uniforms became tattered and the gold lace shredded after a few days in the jungle, being replaced with whatever came to hand, so quickly producing an army of tramps. Highlanders marched to Lucknow during the Mutiny in feather bonnets and white spats; Southern regiments were permitted the concession of a white cap

cover. The last occasion on which British troops went into battle wearing red tunics was at Ginnis in the Sudan, fought on the last day but one of 1885. In India in the mid-1850s, the time-honoured scarlet of the British Army was slowly replaced by khaki, made by dyeing white clothing with coffee, curry-powder or mulberry juice. After the Mutiny it was agreed that the dress was not smart enough and it went out of use for several years, not returning until the late 1870s.

Slowly, the British public learned to appreciate their soldiers and, as the Victorian era drifted slowly to its end at the turn of the nineteenth century, Britons confidently sang of their conviction that their soldiers were more than a match for any foreigners:

> 'And when we say we always won,
> And when they ask us how its done,
> We proudly point to everyone
> Of the soldiers of the Queen.'

This confident jingoistic conviction did not falter in the face of the disasters of the Boer War where the man in the ranks, still a Victorian soldier for a few more months, was fighting and dying well, as he had always done against Sikh and Zulu, Afghan and Fuzzy-Wuzzy.

MUSKETS AND RIFLES

Marlborough and Wellington required a firearm of moderate weight that could be easily carried along poor roads or across country by an average-sized infantryman and, because he was a simple fellow, the weapon and its ammunition, cartridges, balls, powder-containers and wadding had to be almost foolproof so that he could handle them with speed and confidence. Often used under adverse conditions of wind, cold and rain, besides having to withstand the hard knocks of campaigning, it had to be a strong weapon with such sights as it possessed invulnerable to damage, unlikely to jam or to explode in the infantryman's face or to require so much powder that the recoil was too great for him repeatedly to sustain. All these things had to be achieved at low cost and in large numbers. For more than two centuries the British Army used the resulting reasonably serviceable muzzle-loading, black-powder-firing flintlock musket, although it fulfilled only a few of these requirements and was practically useless when it rained because the priming powder in the pan refused to explode when damp. Basically it brought victory to the British infantryman because he handled it in a highly efficient manner. Frequently misfiring, it always threw the bullet high so that during the Sind Campaign of 1843, Sir Charles Napier told his troops: 'The first duty of a soldier is obedience, his second is to fire low.'

Some idea of the capabilities of these muskets can be gained from an opinion voiced by Colonel Hanger in 1814:

'A soldier's musket, if not exceedingly well-bored (as many are) will strike the figure of a man at 80 yards; it may be even at 100; but a soldier must be very unfortunate indeed who shall be wounded by a common musket at 150 yards, provided his antagonist aims at him; as to firing at a man at 200 yards with a common musket, he may as well fire at the moon and have the same hopes of hitting your object. I do maintain and will prove, whenever called on, that no man was ever killed at 200 yards by a common soldier's musket, by the person who aimed at him.'

The hard, bright summer sun of Spain and Portugal striking off massed musket barrels betrayed the movement of troops so that the Light Infantry custom of 'browning' musket barrels was adopted by the majority of infantry units. In the Heavy Cavalry however browning seems to have been universal with the issue of new carbines and pistols in 1796. In 1798 a receipt was sent to all Colonels of Heavy Cavalry for 'renewing the brown colour which may be rubbed off from the barrels of the carbines and pistols lately adopted'.

At the beginning of Queen Victoria's reign the Army was equipped with three types of musket – the Pattern 1802, the India Pattern and the Brown Bess. The Heavy Cavalry were armed with 26 in. barrel carbines and 9 in. barrel pistols, both musket-bore; the

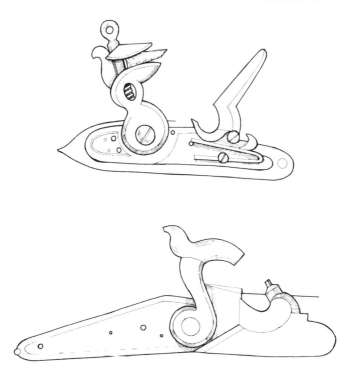

Fig. 12. Above: *Flintlock mechanism, as used on Brown Bess, 1690–1840.* Below: *Percussion mechanism, Brunswick rifle, 1838.*

Light Cavalry had the Paget carbine with a barrel only 16 inches in length and the Paget pistol, both with a ramrod that was linked so as to prevent it being dropped during loading.

Said to be 'successful and well liked', the Pattern 1802 musket was a standardized, smooth-bore musket with a 42 in. barrel, weighing 10 lb. 6 oz.; it fired 'old English Service' round ball fourteen and a half to the pound (commonly known as the ounce bullet). With it was used a socket-fitting, standard 17 in. bayonet.

The India Pattern musket, the weapon of the troops of the Honourable East India Company, weighed 9 lb. 9 oz.; was .75 inches bore and had a barrel 39 inches long.

A gun of destiny bearing the affectionate nickname given by its soldier-owners, for the whole of its existence – the Brown Bess was the finest smooth-bore firearm in any army and was a superb weapon for its day. A brass-mounted musket .75 inches in calibre, it had a 42 in. long barrel and carried a 17 in. bayonet. It was highly suitable for the close-order fighting, the short ranges and the vol-ley-firing of its day and its supersession was sentimentally viewed with regret on all sides.

The Brown Bess cartridge consisted of a tube of stout cartridge paper containing 6 to 8 drams of powder and a lead bullet. Biting off the rear end of the cartridge, the soldier squeezed a small portion of the powder into the flash-pan and emptied the remainder down the barrel; then he inserted the bullet and rammed it with the paper cartridge on top as wadding. Although the loose-fitting bullet limited the range of reasonably accurate fire to some 50 yards, the soldier could fire about two to three rounds per minute, speeded up by pouring the powder into the barrel and dropping the bullet on top of it without the use of wad or ramrod. The charge was then 'firmed home' by banging the butt on the ground which, after shutting his pan, not only consolidated the charge but also sent sufficient powder through the touch hole into the pan to prime the musket, because the powder was fine enough to be used for both primer and charge. In this way the rate of fire was increased from four to five rounds a minute, although frequently insufficient powder reached the pan to allow the musket to fire and the method sadly affected range, accuracy and penetration. Because the only way of unloading a musket with a wadded ball was to discharge it, sentries loaded their arms with 'running ball', i.e. a loose bullet without wadding that could be unloaded by holding the barrel downwards and letting the bullet drop out.

In 1841 the Royal Engineers carried out a test to confirm the capabilities of the Brown Bess. They discovered that, according to the elevation of the barrel, the range varied from 100 to 700 yards with as much as 100 yards variation in the possible range at each elevation. A target about 12 feet high and 3 feet wide was hit three times out of four at 150 yards range; at any greater range no hits at all were scored even with the musket fixed in a rest. A target twice as wide had ten shots fired at it from 250 yards without a single hit being registered. Misfires worked out at one in six and a half shots.

As the Army rapidly reduced in size after 1815, the India Pattern musket and the Brown Bess were gradually dropped in favour of the 1802 Pattern; post-war Waterloo economies caused a wait of about 25 years before the issue of percussion weapons. In this type of weapon, the ignition of the charge within the barrel was caused by the fall of the hammer upon a percussion cap (simply a small copper cylinder lined with fulminating matter) which set fire to the charge by flash through a hollow nipple, obviating priming and making the entire process of loading not only shorter but surer. Sometimes the aperture through the nipple became clogged and had to be cleared with a pricker but far more frequently the channel from the pan to the barrel of the old musket similarly required clearing. Heavy and continuous rain could affect the percussion cap but it was sheltered by letting down the hammer to half-cock and a new cap substituted for the old one in a matter of seconds.

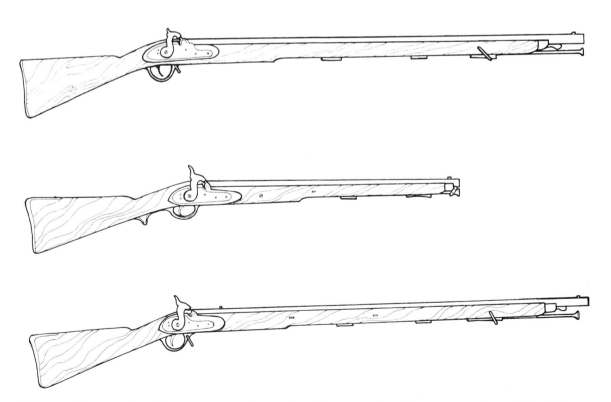

Fig. 13. Above: *1839 Pattern percussion musket.* Centre: *1842 Pattern cavalry carbine.* Below: *1842 Pattern musket.*

13

As a Front Rank:
Prepare to Load.

As a Rear Rank:
Rod.

As a Front Rank
Standing. At......
Yards: Ready.

As a Rear Rank
Standing:
Present (1st Motion).

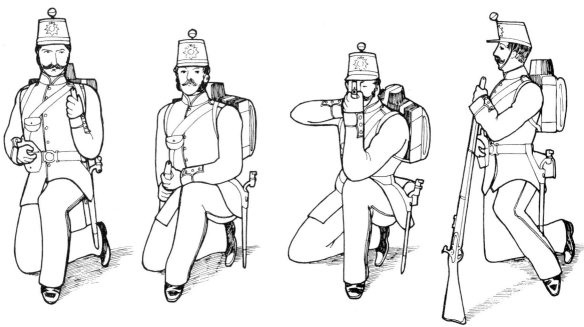

As a Front Rank Kneeling:
Prepare to Re-load.

As a Front Rank Kneeling:
At ...... Yards: Ready.

As a Rear Rank Kneeling:
Present (1st Motion).

As a Rear Rank Kneeling:
Prepare to Re-load.

Prepare for Cavalry: Ready.

Fig. 14. Left: *Positions in the 'Platoon Exercise', or firing drill.* Above: *'Resisting Cavalry'.* (From Company and Battalion Drill 1862.)

The first steps towards re-equipping the Army were taken in 1834 at Woolwich when comparative trials were carried out with flint and percussion locks, invented early in the nineteenth century by the Rev. Alexander John Forsyth of Aberdeenshire. In varying conditions of weather, six flintlock muskets and six percussion muskets fired 6,000 rounds – the flintlock had 922 misfires (one in six and a half), whereas the percussion musket had only thirty-six misses in 6,000 rounds (one in 166); the flint musket scored 3,680 hits; the percussion 4,047. To fire 100 rounds the flint musket required 32 minutes 31 seconds and the percussion 30 minutes 24 seconds.

These impressive results caused the Board of Ordnance to decide to re-equip the Army throughout with percussion arms, a lengthy process that was initially intended to be carried out by utilizing the old flintlocks, but a fire at the Tower of London in 1841 destroyed many thousands of these firearms awaiting conversion. This meant that a new series of arms (Pattern 1842) had to be manufactured. Before that, a percussion version known as Pattern 1839, identical to its flintlock predecessor, except for the altered lock, was used by some units of the British Army, the first occasion in action being by Marines at the capture of Canton in 1841. Pattern 1842 was produced in three barrel lengths – standard length of 39 inches; a lighter version for sergeants with a 33 in. barrel and a 30 in. barrel for the Royal Artillery and the Royal Corps of Sappers and Miners. The Heavy Cavalry were issued with a musket-bore carbine with a 26 in. barrel while the Light Cavalry had a 21 in. weapon of carbine bore. Lancers did not carry carbines because they got in the way of the lance, nor were they carried by sergeant-majors and trumpeters, so a percussion pistol was issued to them with a musket-bore and a 9 in. barrel. Cavalry were ill-served as the pistol was a peculiarly inaccessible weapon – the rider had to remove his right glove, unbutton the flounce, push forward his cloak or draw back the sheepskin and shabracque, and reach for the butt of the pistol concealed under his left arm.

The new weapons represented a revolutionary change if only because for the first time in the history of the Army, the calibre of muskets, carbines and rifles was the same so that one pattern of ammunition served for all. If the old soldiers moaned for the passing of the faithful Brown Bess of their youth, their objections were more than drowned by the welcome given by cavalry, infantry and riflemen to their new weapons. Although the Regular Army handed in its last flintlock somewhere between 1840 and 1850, the 27th Foot in South Africa were still armed with a mixture of flint and percussion muskets in 1846 but two battalions of the 91st were completely equipped with percussion.

A new weapon, the Brunswick rifle, designed by Captain Berners, a Brunswick Jäger officer, was adopted by the Board of Ordnance after trials at Woolwich in 1836. Its calibre was .704 inches; barrel length of 30 inches and sighted to 300 yards, it was fitted with a cross-handled sword-bayonet. Those who had to use it described it as the most unsuitable military weapon ever issued to British troops; J. N. George wrote in his classic work *English Guns and Rifles* (1947) that the Brunswick rifle '. . . was a complete failure . . . rapidly earning the distinction of being regarded as one of the worst arms of its time'. The main faults of the weapon were that the bore was too tight-fitting and there was insufficient power to keep the bullet spinning fast enough for straight flight. During the Kaffir War of 1846–48, the King's Royal Rifle Corps found it so difficult to load that each man was issued with a few rounds of smooth-bore ammunition 'for emergencies'. Reporting on the Brunswick rifle in 1852, a Select Committee on Small Arms said:

'At all distances above 400 yards the shooting was so wild as to be unrecorded. The Brunswick rifle has shown itself to be much inferior in point of range to every other arm hitherto noticed. The loading of this rifle is so difficult that it is a wonder how the Rifle Regiments have continued to use it

so long – the force required to ram down the bore being so great as to render any man's hand unsteady for accurate shooting. Comment is unnecessary.'

Colonel (later General) John Jacob of the Scinde Irregular Horse found that a rifling with four grooves instead of two and a bullet with two cross belts to fit them gave much better results with the Brunswick rifle. However, the East India Company refused to adopt his suggestion that the Brunswick rifle of the Company's armies should be so modified. Jacob continued his experiments with bullets and also had rifles made to his own design, with short barrels of about 24 inches, a calibre of .577 or .524 inches, rifling of four deep grooves and one complete turn in 30 inches. Never officially adopted, these rifles were used quite extensively in the Indian Army; in 1856 Jacob formed the 1st Regiment of Jacob's Rifles and at his own expense equipped them with a double-barrelled rifle of his own design. The bayonet he contrived to go with this weapon having a blade of 30 inches, was the longest ever in use. The guard was like that of a sword, with an elaborate scrolled and pierced bowl, and the double-edged blade form was akin to the Highland broadsword.

It was the tight-fitting bullet that made the loading of rifles so slow and constant experiments sought a missile that could be dropped loosely down the muzzle in the manner of a musket ball and then made to fit tightly after it was in position. The Minié rifle, which allowed this by causing the bullet to expand through the force of the explosion, was tested by the British Government, who purchased the right to use the invention. Called the 'Rifle Musket 1851', the first of the new system were little more than rifled versions of the percussion smooth-bore muskets of 1842. Although a muzzle-loader, it was a great advance upon the old smooth-bore musket, .702 in. in calibre and with a 39 in. barrel, its wide bore allowed a heavy bullet with great smashing power. It was sighted up to 900 yards and, being a long rifle it was effective with a fixed bayonet. Considered to be remarkably accurate, with a white target 6 feet high and 3 feet wide, on the test two hits out of five were obtained at 500–800 yards and one hit out of seven shots at 900 yards.

The Board of Ordnance sent out a limited number of Minié rifles to South Africa for testing during the Kaffir War of 1846–52. They were issued to the six best shots in each infantry company who took readily to the new weapon and on numerous occasions dispersed small bodies of natives at ranges from 1,200 to 1,300 yards, being encouraged by their officers who presented prizes for the best shooting. Except for the 4th Division (who still carried the old smooth-bore musket) all the British Infantry in the Crimea were equipped with the new rifles. They could be loaded quickly and easily so that it was no longer necessary to wildly spray bullets for the sake of speed – with practice, every single soldier could fire accurately. On board the *Ripon* en route to the Crimea, the Grenadier Guards practised firing with their new Minié rifles at a painted-board target hung from the foretop gallant studding sail boom. The most popular target was the life-size Russian soldier painted on canvas that replaced the original target when the sea was calm. But this soon ended when the Grenadiers had to hand over all their practice ammunition to the Rifle Brigade, who sailed from Malta to Constantinople with only thirty rounds per man. It was said at the time that the ammunition was so badly made that it was very doubtful whether it would prove serviceable after a week's rough and frequent usage on the march.

The Minié rifle had only a short career in the British Army because in 1853, after successful trials, the Enfield rifle was put into immediate production at the new Royal Small Arms Factory of Enfield, where they were manufactured by American-made machinery. Issued before the end of the Crimean War, it was first used on active service at Sebastopol. Far in advance of any previous firearms issued to the British Army, the Enfield rifle-musket had a barrel 39 inches in length and a calibre of .577 inches; it was sighted up to 900 yards and it weighed only 8 lb. 14 oz. There were various modifications of the standard type of Enfield – that carried by sergeants had a 33 in. barrel while

the cavalry and other mounted units were armed with Enfield carbines.

The Enfield needed a very close fit of cartridge and ball; in order to be quickly rammed down the barrel the cartridges were encased in greased paper and, after biting off the end, the powder was poured down the barrel and the remainder containing the wad and bullet was forced home with a ramrod. The bullet was also lubricated so as to be smoothly driven down the barrel. It is said that the Enfield rifle was the immediate cause of the Indian Mutiny when a rumour spread throughout the East India Company's Army that the cartridge was lubricated with the grease made from the fat of cows sacred to Hindus and the lard of pigs hated by Mohammedans.

When the Indian Mutiny started some of the mutinous regiments of the Company's Bengal Army were armed with Enfields whereas many of the British regiments (including the 32nd Foot which defended Lucknow) still had the Pattern 1842 smooth-bore muskets. Stationed in Meerut where the Mutiny began, the 60th Regiment did good work with the new weapons having thoroughly mastered them in the four months since their issue. In action, the prone rifleman fired at will when ready, re-loading by turning on to his back: the black powder stung his tongue as he tore away the end-paper of a fresh cartridge with his teeth; then emptying its contents into the rifle, he hammered the butt on the ground. Reversing the rifle, the ball was rammed home, the rifleman fumbling with sore fingers in the cap-pocket for the copper percussion cap, which had to be thumbed home before he was ready to fire again. Trained soldiers rarely wasted a shot, never snatching the trigger; picking their target they aimed low '. . . for his guts'. The standard ammunition issue of ten rounds per man proved woefully inadequate and was quickly improved.

Regiments sent out as reinforcements were equipped with the Enfield, and Private Charles Wickins of the 90th Light Infantry recorded in his Indian Mutiny journal: 'We marched on for a few miles, when the enemy again began to show themselves in force on our right, we opened fire on them and, our

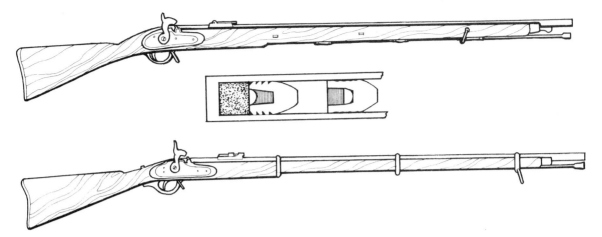

Fig. 15. Above: *Minié Rifle, 1851.* Centre: *Minié bullet.* Below: *Enfield rifle, 1853.*

Enfields being well elevated, we made them move at a distance of 1,200 yards.'

With these new and accurate weapons, a well-trained soldier could fire three shots a minute under good conditions and sustain a rate of two shots a minute in combat. Up to 200 yards, a reasonable marksman could ex-

pect a large percentage of hits, beyond that he could hit a target 6 feet square at 500 yards and a target 8 feet square at least once in every two shots at 1,000 yards. At that distance, the standard ball driven by 60 grains of black powder could penetrate 4 inches of soft pine. However, the new rifle

Fig. 16. A group of officers and other ranks of the 93rd Highlanders outside the barracks at Scutari soon after their arrival in Turkey in 1854. (Photograph by James Robertson.)

Fig. 17. Hand-to-hand fighting at the battle of Isandhlwana during the Zulu War. (Painting by C. E. Fripp.)

Fig. 18. The defenders of Rorke's Drift struggling to rescue wounded comrades from the burning buildings, while others keep the Zulus at bay. (After A. de Neuville, 1880.)

had its limitations as its cylindrical bullet passed clean through a man and sometimes failed to stop a hashish-crazed sepoy, whereas a Minié bullet, its soft leaden nose blunted by being shaved off with a clasp-knife, expanded in flight to cause a wound big enough to put a fist in. Some 50 years later, the International Red Cross decreed that these 'dum-dum' bullets (named after an arsenal near Calcutta) should only be employed against savages – 'to give them an idea of the advantages of civilization' as an old soldier of the time said. Although capable of stopping a charging man in his tracks, these mutilated bullets would not fly true and were only effective at point-blank range.

Now the ordinary infantryman as well as the élite rifleman could fire accurately and in consequence the style of fighting altered as opposing armies were forced to remain further apart than in the past. No longer could the dashing Horse Artillery gallop up to within 300–400 yards of a formation, unlimber and rake it with canister, because the infantrymen with their new weapons could inflict discouragingly high rates of casualties upon the gunners. The Enfield rifle served the British Army well for some years – the official report on the Ambela Expedition of 1863 said:

'Full advantage was taken of the superior range and accuracy of the Enfield rifle and it was clear that the Army in India had made great progress in the conduct of the mountain campaign since the war in Afghanistan of 30 years earlier.'

The Enfield was first used in the hills of the North-West Frontier during the 1858 Expedition against the Khudu Khels where '... its effective fire made a great impression not only on the enemy but also on the native chiefs who accompanied the force'.

During Rose's march to Kalpi in the last stages of the Mutiny, on 7 May 1858 during an action fought in appalling heat, the Enfield rifles were rendered useless by the sun, the men being unable to drive the bullet down into the breech however much strength they used.

In the Maori Wars of 1863 it was said that at the short range at which many of the actions were fought the Maori's double-barrelled muskets were superior to the muzzle-loading Enfield which was slower to load, and soon became faulty because of leading. The reliance placed upon the Enfield in India is indicated by the fact that, during the Bhutan Campaign of 1865, the reserve ammunition of H.M. 80th Foot alone amounted to 500,000 rounds of Enfield ball-cartridges.

During tests at the Hythe School of Musketry in April 1857, a rifle designed by Sir Joseph Whitworth excelled the Enfield musket three to one and displayed remarkable accuracy at more than 1,800 yards. Although used by the Rifle Brigade for a short time, the Whitworth rifle was never adopted as a service firearm because of its serious defect of fouling its bore, but many of them were purchased by the Confederate States of America and used with remarkable results by marksmen during the American Civil War.

In 1855, the Army adopted the Lancaster rifle for limited use and it was issued to 1st Battalion The Rifle Brigade during the Kaffir War. It had a $3\frac{1}{2}$ in. barrel and the same bore of .577 inches as the Enfield, being used with the Enfield cartridge. Later, the Lancaster rifle-musket was adopted as the arm of the Royal Engineers (Corps of Sappers and Miners).

In 1857 the British Army began to test breech-loading carbines of four different patterns – the British-designed Terry and the Westley Richards (used by the 8th Hussars during the Indian Mutiny) and the American Sharps and the Greene. Although the Terry and Sharps were both good weapons and extensively used during the American Civil War, the various British cavalry regiments that tested the carbines found the Westley Richards to be by far the most successful and in 1861 it was approved as the firearm for the cavalry of the Army. But the rest of the Army were still equipped with the muzzle-loading Enfield or (in the case of the Royal Engineers) the Lancaster.

Fig. 19. Above: *The infantry battalion in line.*
Fig. 20. Below: *The infantry battalion in column.*

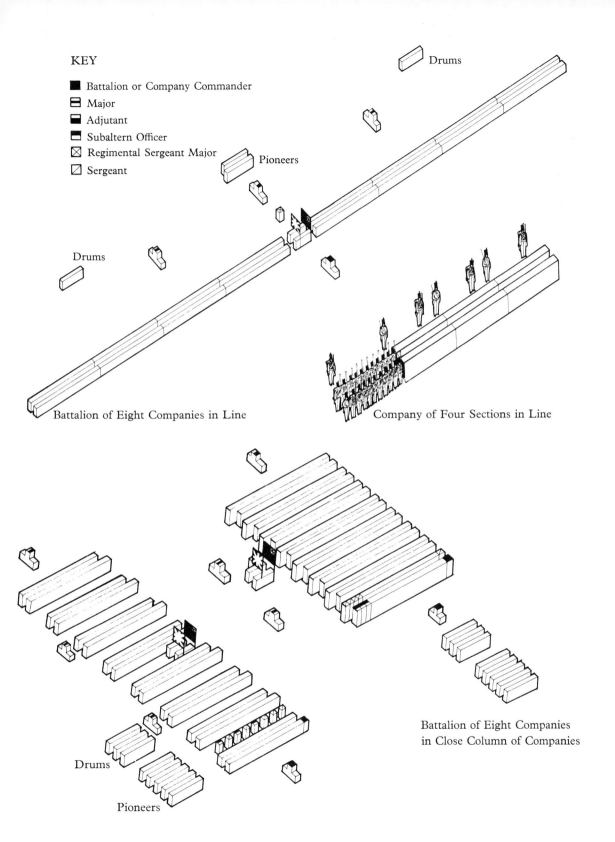

KEY

- ■ Battalion or Company Commander
- ⊟ Major
- ◨ Adjutant
- ⊡ Subaltern Officer
- ⊠ Regimental Sergeant Major
- ▨ Sergeant

Drums

Pioneers

Drums

Battalion of Eight Companies in Line

Company of Four Sections in Line

Battalion of Eight Companies
in Close Column of Companies

Drums

Pioneers

Battalion of Eight Companies in Quarter Column
(Companies at Quarter Intervals)

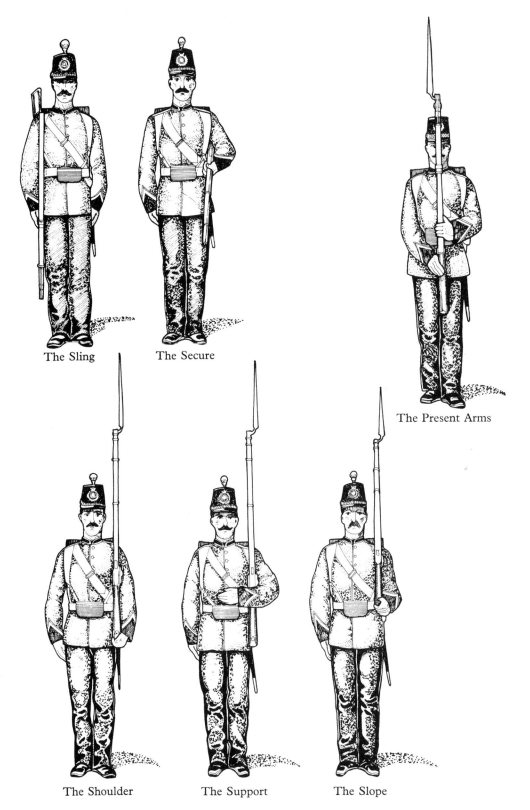

The Sling   The Secure

The Present Arms

The Shoulder   The Support   The Slope

Fig. 21. 'Manual Exercise for the Long Rifle.' Arms drill from Rifle Exercises and Military Instruction, *September 1870.*

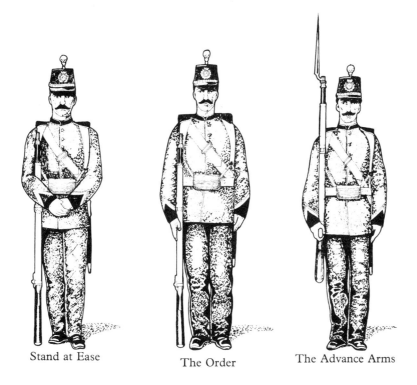

Stand at Ease   The Order   The Advance Arms

The Trail   The Port   The Charge

Superiority of the Prussian Army's bolt-action needle gun during its wars against Denmark in 1864 and Austria in 1866, together with the knowledge that several foreign armies had equipped themselves with breech-loading rifles, made it clear that the muzzle-loader was obsolescent. So a Select Committee was appointed in 1864 to consider equipping the British Army with breech-loaders. Not wishing to waste the large stocks of good muzzle-loading rifle-muskets, the Committee selected the mechanism designed by Jacob Snider of New York which would convert the muzzle-loading Enfields. The Enfield cartridge with its separate cap was found to be unsatisfactory so a centre-fire cartridge was adopted and a claw extractor fitted to the breech mechanism, which partially pulled the cartridge case out of the open breech, to be thrown clear by turning the rifle upside down. In 1865 the Army began to be equipped with this pattern of the Snider–Enfield rifle, which was improved in 1867 by the adoption of Colonel Boxer's improved centre-fire, brass-bodied cartridge.

With the bayonet the Snider rifle was 6 feet $\frac{1}{2}$ inch long; it was loaded at the breech by an opening block working upon a pin, being thrown open by a smart action of the right thumb to receive the cartridge. With great effort, the British troops in the Abyssinian Campaign of 1868 were equipped with the Snider rifles – the first time the breech-loading rifle had been used in the field by the British Army. At Arogi on 10 April 1868, the King's Own Royal Lancaster Regiment checked a headlong charge by a screaming horde of Abyssinian warriors led by mounted chiefs in scarlet robes, the British infantry deploying into two lines and fanning out into skirmishing order before opening fire with their Sniders at 150 yards range. 'How they just about did catch it . . . you never saw such a sight,' gloried Lieut W. W. Scott in his *Letters from Abyssinia during the Campaign of 1868*. By 1869, the rifle had been issued to all the Regular troops and to 16,000 of the Militia. Ably handled by the Black Watch and the Rifle Brigade, the fire-power of the Snider rifle proved the battle-winning factor in the dark jungles of Ashanti in 1874. In the late 1860s a Snider-type carbine was introduced and served until 1877 when it was issued to Yeomanry, Volunteers and the Irish Constabulary; the Regular Cavalry were issued with the Martini–Henry carbine.

The Snider–Enfield conversion was only a stop-gap, and a Board convened to study all available breech-loading systems tested 120 different actions and forty-nine different cartridges before adopting the Martini–Henry in 1871. The Martini–Henry Mark I was issued to the troops in 1874, followed by the Mark II of 1876 and the Mark III of 1879, both embodying minor modifications. The improved rifles were accompanied by a new system of drill, described in 'Field Exercises and Evolutions of Infantry', specially issued in April 1877.

The 1871 Martini–Henry fired a black-powder, .45 calibre, centre-fire, Boxer cartridge of thin rolled brass, with a heavy lead slug weighing 480 grains, paper-wrapped at the base to prevent melting in its passage down the bore. The breech-block was hinged at the rear and dropped to expose the chamber when the lever behind the trigger guard was depressed, flipping out the expanded case. A fresh round was laid atop the grooved block and thumbed home, and the piece was cocked when the lever was raised. There was no safety catch. With the bayonet fixed, the rifle was 5 feet $11\frac{1}{2}$ inches in length ($49\frac{1}{2}$ inches without); it weighed 9 lb.; and it was sighted for shooting at 500 yards when the trajectory of its bullet was 8.1 feet. When a ball left a rifle it rose considerably in the air and fell again in a curve to its destination – thus the bullet rose 8.1 feet in the Martini–Henry; the 11.9 feet of the Snider, and the 15 feet trajectory of the old Enfield indicating the great superiority of the new weapon.

Rudyard Kipling, that redoubtable chronicler of the British soldier, extolled the merits of the Martini–Henry rifle in *The Young British Soldier*:

'When 'arf of your bullets fly wide in the ditch,
Don't call your Martini a cross-eyed old bitch;

She's human as you are – yoo treat her
as sich,
An' she'll fight for the young British
soldier.'

In trained hands the rifle was accurate to a
1,000 yards and more. Battalion volley fire
against massed targets frequently opened at
600 to 800 yards, and even an average marksman could score hits at 300 or 400 yards.
The soft lead slug was a man-stopper that
smashed bone and cartilage and left wicked
wounds.

With its smaller bore, greater range, lower
trajectory and superior accuracy, the
Martini–Henry rifle was far in advance of
any arm previously issued to the British soldier. Its easy operation and quick reloading
gave rise to the claim that it was the earliest
general issue of a shoulder-arm that could
compete successfully with the longbow of
the Hundred Years War so far as range,
rapidity of firing and robustness were concerned – every earlier firearm had been in
some degree inferior to the master weapon of
Crecy, Poitiers and Agincourt.

The simplicity and efficiency of the
Martini–Henry made it one of the best ever
designed but from a military point of view it
suffered from the two very serious defects of
being liable to jamming through sand in the
mechanism (this gave great trouble in the
Egyptian Campaign of 1882), and fouling
lodged readily in the deep and square-cut
grooves of the rifling. The bore was .450
against the .577 inches of the Snider–
Enfield, nevertheless the latter was the more
pleasant weapon to fire for the Martini–
Henry had a vicious kick in its recoil,
especially when the bore was foul; shoulders
were bruised after a few rounds and nose-
bleed was not uncommon. Despite the
protection of a wooden forestock, prolonged
firing soon made the barrel too hot to touch
and during the Zulu War of 1879 the
infantry sewed wet rawhide covers around
the balance, cutting a hole for the rear leaf-
sight after the skin had dried and shrunk.
Even so, this overheating caused considerable trouble at Rorke's Drift:

'Most of the men had fired several
hundred rounds through their scorching
barrels, and the fouled pieces kicked
brutally, lacerating trigger fingers and
pounding shoulders and biceps until they
were swollen and raw. Here and there an
overheated barrel glowed dully in the dark,
cooking off rounds before the men could
raise their guns to fire. The breeches jammed
unless they were unloaded at once; the heat
softened the thin rolled brass, which stuck to
the chamber while the extractor tore the iron
head off the case, and men dug at the open
breeches with their knives to pick out the
empties. Despite the protective wooden fore-
stocks, the barrels blistered palms and
burned finger tips, and the men wrapped
rags around their left hands or sucked at
their fingers and tried to fire with one hand,
resting the guns on the mealie bags.'*

At Abu Klea in 1895 the single-shot
Martini–Henrys, plus a couple of
repeatedly-jamming Gardner guns, in the
hands of Stewart's 1,500 men strewed 1,100
dead Dervishes around the square in a battle
that only lasted five minutes. Even so, it was
recorded that the Martini–Henry rifles
jammed owing to the heat caused by the
rapid firing, so that the men had to fight off
the fanatical Dervishes with the butt and the
bayonet. Until after the adoption of
smokeless powder, the Martini was the principal weapon of the British infantryman and,
with different bores, it took its toll of
Afghans, Afridis, Dervishes, Zulus and a
host of other native tribesmen in innumerable minor Colonial wars. Near Kandahar
during the Afghan War of 1879, a party of
Highlanders allowed attacking natives to
come within 200 yards before driving them
off by heavy file-firing with their Martini–
Henrys. The Sudanese Campaign of 1884–
85 was fought almost entirely with the
Martini–Henry rifle because the primitive
machine-guns frequently jammed and transport difficulties prevented many guns accompanying the force.

At Hasin, two squadrons of Bengal
Lancers were forced to retire on to the
square formed by the Guards, who had been
posted as a reserve in the rear. Racing after

---

* Donald Morris, *The Washing of the Spears*,
Jonathan Cape, London, 1966, p. 414.

Fig. 22. Martini-Henry, mechanism, and bayonet, 1871.

the retiring horsemen the Arabs came suddenly upon this square and, without a moment's hesitation, threw themselves at it. Firing as coolly as if in Hyde Park, the Guards prevented even one of the 2,800 Arab spearmen and riflemen getting nearer than 15–20 yards to the outer fringe of bayonets. During the same battle the Berkshires and the Marines were sent forward to assault the enemy's position; dashing forward in gallant style they made it into a race to reach some hillocks on the right of the ridge occupied by the foe. The Marines were the first to reach the crest of these earthwaves, from which they covered the advance of the Berkshires by well-directed fire, the rolling volleys of musketry echoing among the surrounding hills. Forced from their position on the hills, the Arabs retired across the plain harried by two squadrons of Bengal Lancers.

At Tamai, Buller's square, assailed in a furious manner, had literally blown away all the enemy rushing towards them by sheer fire-power. Seeing that the Dervishes had hit Davis's square, the Gordons, Royal Irish and Rifles poured a steady fire across the open ground at them and masses of the enemy melted away under the terrible fire of the two squares – not a living man could survive against the fire of massed Martini rifles, Gatlings and field guns. The defeat of the Arabs in this part of the field was completed by the cavalry who, sweeping round the left flank, dismounted and poured volley after volley into the retreating foe.

At Matun during the 3rd Afghan War, for the first time the 10th Hussars used the new dismounted exercise, doing excellent shooting at 500 yards with their short Martini–Henry carbines. They were said to have been '. . . as cool and steady as if at target practice on Wormwood Scrubs'. The same unit used these carbines very effectively to cover the retreat from Matun a few days later.

The Martini–Henry was a single-shot weapon and its life was inevitably short as the demand arose for magazine rifles. In 1875 James P. Lee, a Scottish watchmaker who had taken United States citizenship, designed a simple, cheap and efficient box magazine which fitted over a Martini breech, the cartridges feeding in by gravity. The increased fire-rate of the magazine rifle made it necessary for the soldier to carry a greater quantity of ammunition – a problem which could also be solved by reducing the size of the large bore of the Martini–Henry to allow smaller cartridges to be fired. The supply of ammunition for the Martini–Henry rifle played a major part in one of the greatest disasters in British Army history when just before the Battle of Rorke's Drift almost an entire force was wiped out at Isandhlwana during the Zulu War of 1879.

Cartridges for the Martini–Henry came in paper packets of ten rounds; each man carried four packets in the leather ammunition pouches on his belt, ten loose rounds in a small canvas expense pouch and two additional packets tucked into his knapsack. On

26

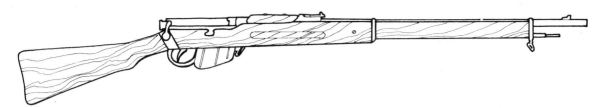

Fig. 23. Lee-Metford rifle, 1888.

the march a battalion carried a regimental reserve of fifty boxes (enough to provide thirty extra rounds per man) packed into two waggons or three carts. A field reserve of 480 rounds per man travelled in the waggons of the supply train. The sturdy wooden boxes held 600 rounds; they were 2 feet long, 7 inches wide and 9 inches deep; full, they weighed 80 lb., and were equipped with rope handles at either end. The lids were held down by two strong copper bands, each secured with nine stout screws.

The usual routine was for the men to be woken just before dawn, to fall-in and stand-to arms until the sun rose. Then the quarter-masters mustered at the Regimental ammunition reserve waggons to issue haversacks filled with paper packets each containing ten rounds which were distributed to the men. On 22 January 1879 at Isandhlwana when the bugles brought the men tumbling out of their tents on the approach of the Zulus, they were wearing belts with forty rounds in the pouches but few carried their haversacks with the extra two packets and some had discarded their expense pouches holding the loose ten rounds. Consequently most of the men went into battle with only forty to fifty rounds, soon expended in half an hour's firing, so that drummer-boys and bandsmen were soon racing back for fresh packets of cartridges. The quartermasters of the 1st and 2nd Battalions 24th Foot were doling out packages of bullets at the two battalion ammunition waggons in the transport lines. Each closely scrutinized the messengers to ensure that they were at the correct waggons because after the fight, every cartridge would have to be accounted for as expended; even the boxes themselves were accountable. For these reasons only one box was opened at a time. Using screwdrivers, the quartermasters had begun to loosen the screws on at least one of the boxes early in the fight, so as to be ready as soon as demands came from the firing line. Six screws, frequently rusted into the wood and hard to start, had to be removed to raise the lid.

Because the 2nd Battalion waggon was closest to the fighting, all the messengers clamoured around it loudly demanding cartridges – the 'unentitled' were sent to the second waggon 500 yards further on. Messengers from the Natal Native Horse were refused cartridges by both quartermasters, because they were not their responsibility! Lieut Smith-Dorrien (one of the few survivors who later became a General) ordered a party of men to prise open the boxes in the 1st Battalion's field reserve waggon. Donald Morris again describes the scene:

'There were no extra screwdrivers, and it was slow work. Chelmsford had requisitioned spare ones for this very purpose, but the order was lost somewhere in Natal. The men hacked at the copper bands with axes or thrust bayonets under them and attempted to snap them or prise them up over the screw heads. Smith-Dorrien finally worried one of the boxes open and began to thrust handfuls of the precious packets into the helmets and haversacks that were eagerly held up to him. The quartermaster, working in the Regimental reserve waggon nearby, looked up and saw him. He was horrified. "For heaven's sake don't take that, man," he yelled, "it belongs to our battalion!" Smith-Dorrien snarled back, "Hang it all, you don't want a requisition now, do you?" and continued to dole out the packets.

A trickle of ammunition was starting out to the companies, but it was not enough. More and more men were coming back in desperation, searching the waggons until they found the familiar crates and pounding the boxes apart with stones when they found

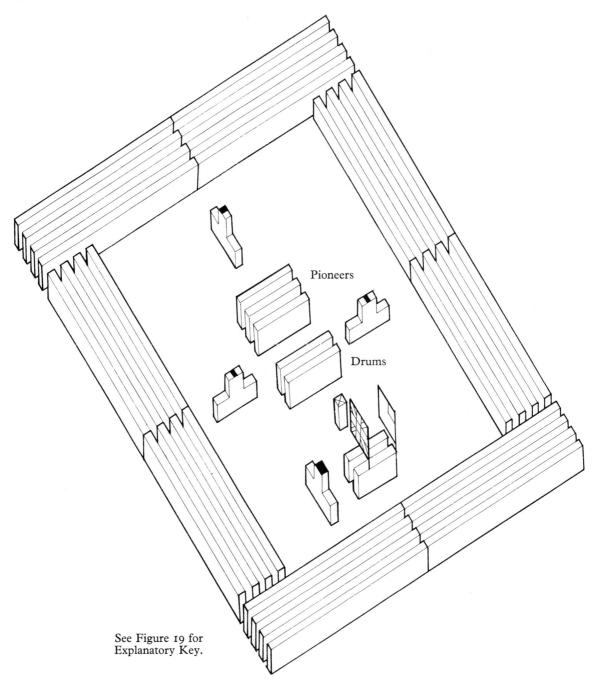

Pioneers

Drums

See Figure 19 for
Explanatory Key.

Fig. 24. The infantry battalion of eight companies in square formation.

them. The fire in the line began to slacken.'*

Freed from the terrible fire that had pinned them down, the Zulus leapt to their feet and charged forward, pouring through a gap left by the panic-stricken flight of Natal Kaffirs. Out of ammunition, the outnumbered British infantry fought bravely with bayonet and butt for a few minutes before being overwhelmed by the ferocity of the Zulus. At Isandhlwana 1,300 British and Native troops were killed but not before the Martini–Henrys had exacted 2,000 Zulu casualties.

* Donald Morris, *The Washing of the Spears*, Jonathan Cape, London, 1966, p. 373.

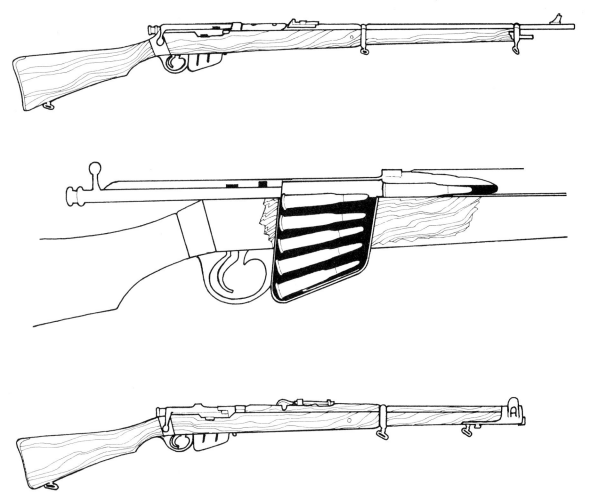

Fig. 25. Above and centre: *Lee-Enfield rifle, 1895.* Below: *Short magazine Lee-Enfield.*

During the same year, at the bitterly contested defence and relief of Kam Dakka on the North-West Frontier of India, so much ammunition was expended that it began to run out and the troops received orders to cease firing except when the enemy came within 150 yards, otherwise they were to await an assault with fixed bayonets. Fire-discipline became an important factor in warfare – at Metamneh in the Sudan in 1885, the infantry square halted to receive a fierce charge of Dervishes; the men gave vent to their feelings in wild spontaneous cheering then set to work firing as they would have done at an Aldershot field-day. Seeing that the fire was having little effect, the bugle sounded 'cease fire' and surprisingly the men obeyed the call. The momentary rest steadied them and when the enemy got to

within about 300 yards they recommenced firing with deadly effect; all the leaders with their fluttering banners went down and not a single native got within 50 yards of the square.

In the 1880s, the size of a bullet could not be reduced because the muzzle velocity of the rifles did not give the bullet sufficient 'stopping power', particularly against tough native foes such as Dervishes. The required stopping power could be obtained by a smaller bullet if the velocity was increased, an impossibility because the lead bullets were too soft to be propelled at a faster rate down the barrel. Rubin, a Swiss Artillery Officer, realized that a smaller and lighter bullet was the only way to increase velocity, with a subsequently flatter trajectory, greater accuracy and longer range; merely to increase the charge for the larger bullet would only produce an unbearable recoil. Rubin designed a .295 in. lead bullet (compared with the Martini–Henrys .450) and encased it in a sheath of copper capable of standing up to the stress and friction in the barrel. The reduced diameter of the bullet caused the cartridge to be long and thin, so Rubin designed a brass cartridge case with a narrowed-down neck that tightly held the copper-encased bullet in place. In 1887 the British experimented with the Rubin rifle of .30 inches and in the following year the calibre of British Army rifles was reduced to .303 inches – which is still the standard for all full-bore, bolt-action rifles.

During the Chitral Campaign of 1895 the Scottish Borderers, linked arm-in-arm, forded the Swat River opposite a small fort which they carried under cover of the mountain guns; the Sikhs crossed in like fashion lower down and occupied two villages. This arm-linking method of river crossing was only possible with the brass cartridges and breech-loading rifles, in the old days of paper cartridges the musket and pouch had to be held above water.

When the calibre of British Army rifles was reduced to .303 inches, the increased velocity was initially obtained by using a charge of compressed black powder but as the British Army (in common with other nations) changed to the small-calibre, high-velocity bullet, it sought a smokeless propellant so as to eliminate the revealing cloud of smoke that issued from the muzzle of a rifle when a black powder-filled cartridge was fired. In Europe, Alfred Nobel a Swedish engineer who had invented dynamite, subsequently discovered that nitrocellulose and nitroglycerine in equal proportions formed ballistite, capable of being manufactured in grains and used for cartridges. Then Britain perfected a method of producing cordite from nitroglycerine and gun-cotton gelatinized and blended together with acetone and a mineral jelly to give stability in different climates. Cordite, when hardened and processed into long spaghetti-like threads, could be cut into cartridge-lengths and, from 1892, the new British Service small-arms ammunition had an increased velocity of 2,000 feet per second compared to the 1,800 per second of the compressed black-powder charge.

No more would the British soldier find himself in a situation as at Tamai in 1884 when the frantic attack of the Dervishes towards the square caused the infantry to feverishly blaze away so that neither bugle calls nor orders could persuade them to reserve their fire or to aim steadily. Within half a minute the square was blinded by the dense smoke of its own rifles allowing the enemy to creep up the rocky side of the ravine and hundreds of the dark, demon-like figures burst out of the haze of dust and smoke upon the right-angle of the square, crawling in on hands and knees, cutting and stabbing. Scuttling beneath the bayonets and muzzles of the Gatling and Gardner guns, they broke into the square to force it back in wild confusion, until the infantry rallied to throw back the courageous Dervishes.

In 1877 James Lee brought out his bolt-action breech and box magazine which served the British Army for 70 years before being replaced by semi-automatic mechanisms. In 1888, the British adopted Lee's idea with an improved magazine and a rifle barrel of .303 in. calibre, designed by an Englishman, William Ellis Metford. Known as the Lee–Metford, this rifle had a magazine fitted beneath the breech, basically the same as the type used by most armies in both world wars. The first magazine of the Lee–Metford held eight rounds of the black-powder ammunition, increased to ten rounds when cordite ammunition was introduced.

Kitchener's Omdurman campaign was fought by infantry armed with Lee–Metford rifles, their magazine holding five rounds inserted separately as chargers were not then in use. The pencil diameter Lee–Metford bullet, drilling a hole even through bone, did not always stop or bring down on-rushing fanatics such as the Dervish or North-West Frontier tribesman. Nevertheless its effectiveness was demonstrated at the Battle of Omdurman on 2 September 1898, when the Lee–Metfords of the Grenadier Guards opened fire on the charging Dervishes with section-volleys at 2,000 yards and stopped them 500 yards from the British position.

Then, as the Dervishes edged rightward, the fire ran along to the Highlanders, the Lincolns and then to the Egyptian brigades. The British stood up in double rank behind their zariba, the Egyptians lay down in their shelter trench, both pouring out death as fast as they could load and press the trigger; shrapnel whistled and the Maxims growled savagely. The hot and dry British, Egyptian and Sudanese infantry, deaf in the din and blind in the smarting smoke, fired repeatedly. Rifles grew so hot that men had to change them for others taken from the supports and the water in the jackets of the Maxims boiled furiously. At about 800 yards, fire blazed out deafeningly along the whole line of infantry.

Kitchener put every man in the firing-line, relying upon the destructive effect of modern rifle fire sweeping across the gently rising plain over which the natives attacked. Only time, ammunition and the strength to point the weapon was needed to kill them off. The Dervishes were superb as, mangled by every kind of death and torment that man could devise, they clung round their black and green flags, bravely firing their poor, rotten, home-made cartridges while their spearmen charged hopelessly. A dusky line got up and stormed forward to bend, break up, fall apart and disappear, but before the smoke had cleared another line was storming forward in the same path. The horsemen leading each attack rode into a hail of fire until nothing was left but three horses trotting up to the British line. It was a supreme instance of the futility of gallantry without up-to-date weapons.

At 11.30 in the morning, Kitchener shut his glasses and remarked that the enemy had been given 'a good dusting' by the 22,000-strong Anglo-Egyptian Army, at a cost of 48 killed and 382 wounded. In a welter of blood that turned a battle into an execution, the 40,000-strong Dervish force was wiped out as hardly an army has been destroyed in the history of warfare, losing 11,000 killed, 16,000 wounded and 4,000 prisoners. Had the Allies done the same proportional damage at Waterloo, barely a single Frenchman would have escaped!

Earlier in the same campaign, Atbara was

a victory gained in less than 40 minutes of actual fighting against a horde of half-starved and ill-armed savages who withstood an hour and a half of shell and shrapnel, then volley after volley of blunted Lee–Metford and Martini bullets, delivered coolly at 300 yards and less (the Warwicks were reported to have been 'volleying off the blacks as your beard comes off under a keen razor') and with case-shot and Maxim at almost point-blank range. The guns fired 1,500 rounds, mostly shrapnel; the Camerons averaged thirty-four rounds per man. Yet the natives stood firm in their trenches and never moved until the British soldiers and their comrades surged right on top of them yelling, shooting and bayoneting. Many died where they were, only praying that they might first kill a soldier; those who ran ran slowly, turning doggedly to fire; the wounded had to be killed because they were still dangerous even when nearly dead. Those who escaped had 30 miles of desert to struggle across before they could reach water and safety; for the wounded the desert was certain death. The Dervish losses are unknown but the number of their killed was estimated at forty Emirs and 3,000 men – no less than 2,500 corpses were counted in and near the zariba.

In many respects, the heavy Martini-Henry bullet of the Egyptian Army was superior at close quarters to the Lee–Metford, but the .450 Martini rifle had no magazine and its rate of fire was slow. Even in the years before Omdurman, the re-formed and re-equipped Egyptian Army discovered that their hard-hitting Martini-Henrys were too much for the Dervishes. In 1896, the Dervish character had not altered appreciably and they retained all their old dash and fire, but their spears and Remington rifles were no match for the modern weapons of Kitchener's army.

In the early 1890s the Martini–Metford rifle was evolved from a conversion of the Martini action rifle, with the Metford barrel substituted for the Henry; a large number of the Martini–Henry cavalry carbines and artillery carbines were similarly converted. In 1895 the Metford barrel was modified at Enfield and resulted in the Lee–Enfield rifle; the same barrel was used with Martini-

Fig. 26. Officers and men of the Cameron Highlanders forming square in Egypt, 1882.

Henry rifles and carbines to become the Martini–Enfield rifle. At the start of the Boer War Colonial troops were armed with this weapon and the Indian Army used it until 1905. In 1896 the magazine Lee–Enfield cavalry carbine was introduced but the artillery continued to carry the single-shot Martini action carbine.

The British style of warfare against native foes had taken on an irresistible pattern through the power of the new weapons placed in the hands of the soldier. When the Buner Field Force attacked the Tanga Pass in 1898, the artillery opened fire at 2,200 yards range, covering the Buffs as they made a difficult climb up on to a ridge from where they commenced volley firing at 1,500 yards. The remainder of the infantry made a frontal attack up steep slopes concealing tribesmen positioned behind stone sangars, making steady progress in the face of matchlock fire and avalanches of rocks rolled down upon them. Fast becoming demoralized by the artillery fire and long-range volleys from the Buffs, the tribesmen took to their heels when the attacking infantry neared the top of the slope. Only one man, of the Highland Light Infantry, was killed; the tribesmen lost at least fifty.

In the same year, of the battle of Atbara a war correspondent wrote: 'The men knelt down – "volley-firing by sections" and at exactly the same time firing crashed out from both sides. Overhead the bullets piped wht-t, wht-t, whit-t. Aiming steadily, the Highlanders' volleys crashed out; then a bugle again and everyone was up and on with the bullets swishing and lashing now like rain on a pond. But the line of khaki and purple tartan never bent or swayed – it just went slowly forward with the officers strolling unconcernedly at its head; it was almost as though the pipes picked the men up and carried them on – it was difficult not to hurry but their forward movement was done in orderly and grave fashion. The bullets whispered to raw youngsters in one breath the secret of all the glories of the British Army.'

At first the magazine was regarded as a reserve and the rifles were fitted with a device which slid across to cut the magazines off from the chamber, then the rifle was loaded by hand with a single round after each shot. Presumably this was to prevent the rifle being used too freely because its high rate of fire caused problems of ammunition supply in the field. At Omdurman one British regiment heard behind them a

Fig. 27. Men of the Lincolnshire Regiment awaiting the Dervish attack at Omdurman, 2 September 1898. (From an album belonging to Private R. Kempston.)

familiar voice crying out 'Cease fire please! Cease fire! Cease fire! What a dreadful waste of ammunition!' . . . and Kitchener rode past.

Nevertheless, slowness of re-charging was discovered to be a handicap in the early days of the Boer War until a charger invented by Lee enabled five rounds to be loaded simultaneously. The same war demanded fire-action by mounted troops but their Martini carbines were a very ineffective weapon compared with the magazine Lee–Enfield of the infantry. After the war, carbines were abolished and one pattern of rifle was provided for the whole Army – the Short Magazine Lee–Enfield, known to generations of soldiers in World Wars I and II as the S.M.L.E. The mid-nineteenth century saw a spate of invention and development in barrels, locks, breech mechanisms, rifling, cartridges, explosives, magazines and quick-loading devices. These innovations followed each other so rapidly as to place a new and superior weapon in the hands of the infantryman every 15 or 20 years. Amid all this change, it is to the great credit of British craftsmen that the .303 Short Lee–Enfield rifle proved itself to be the best of its kind on many battlefields so that, with slight modifications, it was in general service from 1895 until the end of World War II.

Today, when the estimated casualties of a nuclear war run into tens of millions, it is pardonable to view with scant respect the weapons of the Victorian soldier. Nevertheless Omdurman, the last major campaign of the century, proved that the small arms and artillery of the British Army of that era were capable of exacting a heavy toll from its enemies.

THE BAYONET

During the Victorian era it was generally accepted that irregular foes such as tribesmen, however brave, hated cold steel and would be dispersed by bayonet charges. This was certainly true at Arogi during the Abyssinian Campaign of 1868 and in numerous typical affrays on the North-West Frontier like the expedition against the Khudu Khels in 1858 when '. . . the enemy were encountered and driven from their position by a bayonet charge'. While in Australia, at Eureka Stockade in 1854, the home-made pikes of the diggers very momentarily crossed with the bayonets of the attacking soldiers, who were later accused of bayonetting wounded men. However, records frequently indicate that fighting hand-to-hand with cold steel, British soldiers were no match for powerful savages such as Zulus and Dervishes who would dodge the bayonets or turn them aside on their shields and then deliver two or three spear thrusts before the wielder of the bayonet could recover. The physique and natural fitness of warrior-enemies made them a tough proposition at close-quarters, so that every effort was made to dislodge or disperse them by the superior and disciplined fire-power of the British troops. It was not always so, one reads of Highlanders at Atbara:

'. . . a line of khaki and dark tartan blending to purple, flashing bayonets at the slope, and set two-month-bearded faces straining towards the zariba; their pipes screamed battle . . . now began the killing as with bul-

let and bayonet and butt, the whirlwind of Highlanders swept on; Seaforths and Lincolns deployed right and left and swept straight across . . . ramming bayonets into bodies until the hilt came up against the flesh with a sickening thud, and then throwing them off to make room for another, like a farm labourer forking hay'. Similarly, at Tel el Kebir in 1882 not a single shot was fired by the British infantry as they advanced, in the semi-darkness of dawn, upon the Egyptian entrenchments. On the left the Highland Brigade went forward more quickly and were first into the enemy position where they fought grimly with bayonet and rifle butt while, on the extreme right, the Irish regiments screamed wildly as they rushed in with the bayonet.

During the 150 years leading up to 1900, inventors introduced or the various Masters-General of Ordnance commissioned many experimental firearms each with a standard bayonet or the inventor's idea of the best bayonet to go with his weapon. Few of these experimental bayonets ever got beyond the trial stage, perhaps the strangest ever to be approved by the Small Arms Committee in 1871 was the Elcho, as a variant to the pattern of 1853 for use on the Snider rifle. It had a spear-shaped blade 21 inches in length and about 10 inches of its back edge was a cross-cut saw, as with the Pioneer's sword of 1856. It was not a great success, trying as it did to combine too many functions into one weapon and although it was revived in 1895 and fitted to the Martini–Henry, Lee–Metford and Lee–Enfield rifles, its previous lack of success was repeated.

The very first 'war' of Victoria's reign, the revolt of 1837 in Canada, was notable for considerable use of the bayonet by the Royals on rebels defending houses at St Charles and by the Royal Scots when they stormed the church at St Eustache. Still carrying the flintlock musket, the ordinary infantryman was issued with a new type of socket-bayonet in 1839 and in 1842 there was an improvement to the spring catch which locked the bayonet even more securely to the muzzle. These early Victorian soldiers knew how to use such weapons – in the Sind Campaign of 1843 at Meani and Dubba, Napier's force of 2,200 including only 500 British infantry, caused 12,000 Baluchi casualties during repeated bayonet charges.

Sir Hugh Gough firmly believed that the eventual issue of a battle 'must be brought to the arbitrament of musketry and the bayonet'. In command at Maharajpore in 1843 and during the two Sikh Wars of 1845–46

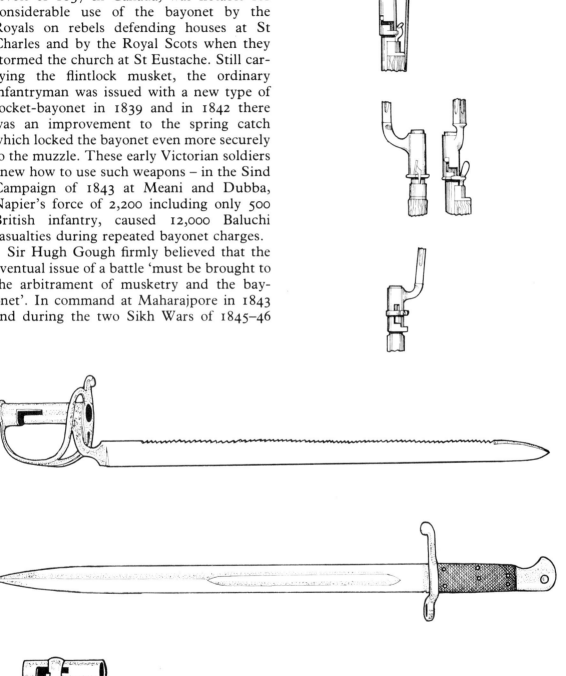

Fig. 28. From top to bottom: *Socket bayonet fittings, 1839, 1842 and 1853, sappers and miners sword; socket bayonet with saw-tooth edge; sword bayonet for the Martini–Henry rifle, 1886; socket bayonet, 1853.*

and 1849, he always preferred the bayonet to musketry or artillery fire. It is recorded that when told at Sobraon that ammunition for the heavy guns had run out, he showed no sign of hesitation or alarm. To the surprise of the officer who brought the message, Gough cried out:

'Thank God! Then I'll be at them with the bayonet!'

Perhaps he gauged the enemy better than did his critics, because Hookhum Singh, a Sikh gunner at Sobraon wrote:

'... who could withstand such fierce demons, with those awful bayonets, which they preferred to their guns – for not a shot did they fire the whole time ...'

Like the Baker rifle, the Brunswick could be fired with bayonet fixed, but due to the length and weight of the bayonet accuracy must have been extremely doubtful. The Brunswick rifle had four different types of bayonet through its fifteen-year life and the first of these, the 'experimental' Pattern –/36, was a curious mixture of the second model Baker sword-bayonet with a 25 in. double-edged sword blade. The unwieldiness of the long blade was obvious and its length was reduced to 17 inches. This caused so many complaints that it was superseded by the pattern of 1837 with the blade lengthened to 22 inches and the fixing device amended so that the cross-guard was completely clear of any muzzle blast, which often tore the bayonet off the rifle or broke the cross-guard, particularly with the Baker rifle. The final bayonet for the Brunswick came in 1848, and had an improved locking and releasing stud which was found to be so effective that it was adopted by the Board of Ordnance.

The Minié rifle had a smaller diameter barrel than the 1842 musket and it was first intended to shrink the socket of the old bayonet to fit the new weapon but, in January 1852, a month before the first issues were to be made, conversion of the 1842 Pattern bayonet was stopped and a new design was adopted. This had a socket and an improved blade with an equi-angular section and three hollowground faces instead of one flat and two hollowground. The Duke of Wellington, then in his last year as Commander-in-Chief, particularly liked the new bayonet and Lord

Hardinge, his successor, was also sufficiently impressed to adopt it as the standard bayonet for all future firearms, to the delight of the infantry who had taken to the new blade. The first universal bayonet ever issued to the British Army went with the 1853 Pattern Enfield rifle and retained the equi-angular hollowground blade of the Minié bayonet so that scabbards were not ordered as the blade fitted into the previous issue. Included was a locking-ring, copied from the French, which replaced the spring catch and held the bayonet securely on the muzzle so that it could neither fall off or be wrenched free by an enemy. Utilized on the Snider rifle (which was an adaptation of the Enfield) this bayonet had an extremely long life and eventually had the socket bushed to fit the Martini–Henry rifle of 1871, not being superseded until 1876, when the socket design remained the same and the length of the blade increased from 17 to 21½ inches.

Called by the troops 'the lunger', the old triangular bayonet played a big part in the fierce hand-to-hand fighting at the defence of Rorke's Drift when the Zulus were repeatedly thrown back from the mealie-bag barricade by bayonet and rifle butt. These bayonet v. assegai duels are very graphically portrayed, perhaps with some licence, in the film *Zulu*.

At Matun, during the 2nd Afghan War 1878, General Roberts sent out his infantry in skirmishing order with cavalry on their flanks and they took each village in turn, '... ferreting out with the bayonet those tribesmen who had hidden in the houses'. Typical of the strength, courage and vigour of native opponents was the fighting around Paimal at the Battle of Kandahar when the 72nd Highlanders and Sikhs desperately fought tribesmen amid walled enclosures. The fanatical Ghazis hurled themselves upon the infantry, dashing shields against bayonets and grappling with the men as they strove to wrench their rifles from their hands.

Disturbing reports from Egypt and the Sudan indicated that the British bayonet Pattern 76 had been found wanting in action, just as the cavalry troopers' swords Patterns 64 and 82 had failed their users. Mr

Fig. 29. *The 3rd Battalion Grenadier Guards engaged with the Russians at bayonet point during the battle of Inkerman, 5 November 1854. (Painting by E. Armitage, R.A.)*

Fig. 30. *'Here's to you Fuzzy-wuzzy.' British infantry holding off a Dervish attack at Abu Klea, 1895. (Painting by W. B. Wollen.)*

Dawnay, the Surveyor-General of Ordnance, aroused fierce Press criticism with the statement that '...the weapons had stood the tests to which they had been put exceedingly well'.

The British infantry fighting in the Sudan probably did feel let down by their bayonets in the fierce mêlées of that campaign and there was little doubt that the bayonets were bad. Mostly imported weapons they were, like the swords, case hardened. Subsequent regrinding or even deep polishing had removed the hardened shell and left a blade that could be easily bent and twisted. Consequently, an English factory capable of supplying Government orders for bayonets was set up by the Wilkinson Sword Company who encountered immediate difficulties in obtaining machinery and skilled labour. Skilled instructors and tools had to be imported from Solingen in Germany and German patents acquired for locking-bolts. This caused a question to be raised in Parliament which imputed that the bayonets, far from being made in England, were in fact being imported once again from Germany. That this was false was borne out by the contents of Government White Paper No. C.5607 published in 1888, which completely vindicated the Wilkinson Sword Company and eventually led to the country having a factory that could and did produce over $2\frac{1}{2}$ million sword-bayonets during World War I.

Even with inferior weapons the British soldier, as always, acquitted himself well as at Abu Klea where Arab spear was met by the unreliable bayonet to a background of short sharp exclamations and brief shouts or oaths as the soldiers engaged with their foes. The Dervishes who reached the square ran on to the serried bayonets of the British ranks, sometimes seizing them in their bare hands and attempting to detach them from the rifles. With a 'hop, skip and a jump' one Arab cleared the front rank, only to be caught on the point of the bayonet by a soldier behind. 'How's that, sir?' said the soldier, turning to his officer. The officer replied: 'Well caught!'

In 1886 and 1887, new pattern sword-bayonets with $18\frac{1}{2}$ in. blades were introduced for the Martini–Henry rifle and the sword-bayonet Pattern –/88 came in with the Lee-Metford rifle in 1888. This rifle was larger than the weapon it succeeded so its bayonet was able to be shortened to only 12 inches without detracting from the effective length of the combined weapon. The Pattern –/88 Mark II was brought into service in 1895 for the Lee–Enfield rifle but differed only very slightly from the original.

During the earlier part of the nineteenth century, Artillerymen and Engineers were issued with special bayonets. In 1875, when the Royal Artillery were given the Martini–Henry, they were still treated differently so far as their bayonet was concerned, as their new sword-bayonet had a blade 18 inches long with about 8 inches of the back edge ground to a cross-cut saw and in 1879 the blade was lengthened to $25\frac{3}{4}$ inches. In 1841, the Engineers had their own bayonet which, like the artillery bayonet, had a saw-back and a socket so designed as to be usable as a grip. It was soon replaced by the Sappers and Miners bayonet Pattern –/43 with a plain blade and no handguard to the grip. The Lancaster carbine was issued to Engineers in 1855 and with it went a special bayonet with a 24 in. blade. The British Army dropped all saw-backed weapons in 1903.

The appearance of a length of shining steel extending from the end of a rifle must produce a certain psychological shock-reaction in the man who has to face it. The better trained and disciplined he is the less effect it will have upon him. Similarly, the high-moraled British soldier of the Victorian era was trained to be aware that bullets would not always bring victory and that he had to be prepared to meet the enemy at bayonet range – only by being willing to fight to the finish assisted by his $21\frac{3}{4}$ in. bayonet for that strip of land would he beat a brave foeman.

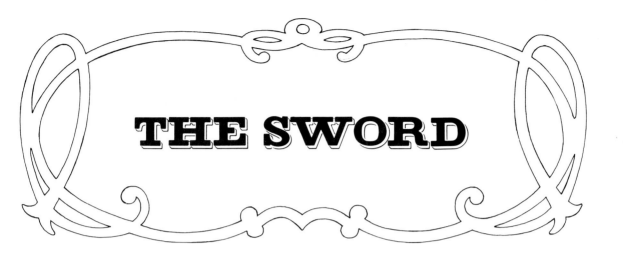

THE SWORD

Throughout history the cavalryman's principal weapon has been the sword – *l'arme blanche*. There were few in the Victorian era who would dispute the necessity of the sword as part of the cavalryman's equipment although the more enlightened maintained that it should be a cutting rather than a thrusting weapon. Like most European cavalry, the British were taught to charge with the point of the sword whereas Eastern cavalry sharpened their tulwars so that they would 'split a hair'. Captain L. E. Nolan – who later became known for carrying the order which caused the ill-fated charge of the Light Brigade at Balaclava – in his book *Cavalry; its History and Tactics* mentioned that he had read a medical report of an engagement in which the Nizam of Hyderabad's Irregular Horse had defeated a superior force of Rohillas, and had been astonished at the havoc created by their swords: heads and arms completely severed, hands cut off at a single blow, and legs above the knee. Was this the work of giants, or of some peculiar quality in the sword blade or its use? The answer surprised him. The swords turned out to be merely old blades discarded by British dragoons, cut to a razor edge and worn in wooden scabbards from which they were never drawn except in action. He inquired the secret of the cavalrymen's skill, and was struck by the simplicity of the reply. 'We never teach them any way, Sir: a sharp sword will cut in anyone's hand,' said one of the Nizam's seasoned troopers.

The lesson of sharp swords was one that Nolan never forgot; it made him contemptuous of cavalry actions where men survived a multiplicity of wounds, when one stroke alone should have been sufficient to cause fatality.

Sergeant Forbes-Mitchell of the 93rd Highlanders, in his *Reminiscences of the Great Mutiny*, recounts the story of the 14th Light Dragoons in action against the Sikhs at Ramnuggur:

'The Sikhs wore voluminous thick puggeries round their heads, which our blunt swords were powerless to cut through, and each horseman had also a buffalo-hide shield slung on his back. They evidently knew that the British swords were blunt and useless, so they kept their horses still and met the British charge by laying flat on their horses' necks, with their heads protected by the thick turban and their backs by the shields; immediately the British soldiers passed through their ranks the Sikhs swooped round on them and struck them back-handed with their sharp, curved swords, in several instances cutting our cavalrymen in two. In one case a British officer was hewn in two by a back-handed stroke which cut right through an ammunition pouch, cleaving the pistol bullets right through the pouch and belt, severing the officer's backbone, and cutting his heart in two from behind.'

Louis Nolan wrote of the same action:

'At Ramnuggur . . . the troopers of the light cavalry had no confidence in their

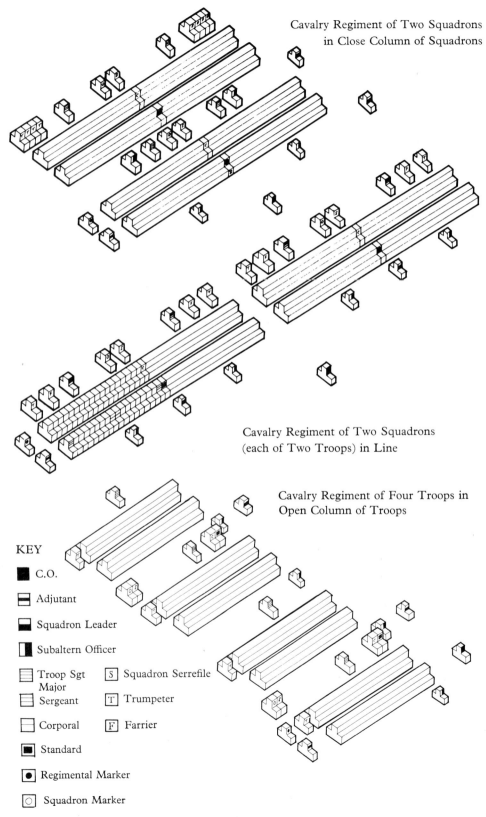

Cavalry Regiment of Two Squadrons
in Close Column of Squadrons

Cavalry Regiment of Two Squadrons
(each of Two Troops) in Line

Cavalry Regiment of Four Troops in
Open Column of Troops

KEY

■ C.O.

▬ Adjutant

▬ Squadron Leader

▐ Subaltern Officer

▤ Troop Sgt
Major

▤ Sergeant

☐ Corporal

■ Standard

◉ Regimental Marker

○ Squadron Marker

S Squadron Serrefile

T Trumpeter

F Farrier

Figs. 21 and 22. Above and below: Formations of the cavalry regiment, 1844.

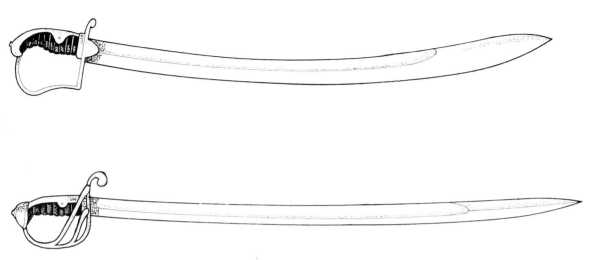

Fig. 33. Light cavalry other ranks sabres. Above: *1796 Pattern.* Below: *1829 Pattern.*

swords . . . a regulation sword in his hand, which must always be blunted by the steel scabbard in which it is encased. The natives' sword-blades were chiefly old dragoon blades cast from our service . . . they all had an edge like a razor from heel to point, were worn in wooden scabbards . . . are never drawn except in action.'

It is not unreasonable to state that most of the patterns of swords issued to British cavalrymen in the nineteenth century were poor in that they possessed almost every fault that a sword could have. They were too short, too heavy, too blunt and apt to turn in the hand so that in the excitement of an action the cut, as often as not, was made with the flat. Perhaps the finest sword ever used by British cavalry was the light cavalryman's sword of 1796, a curved weapon $32\frac{1}{2}$–33 inches in length with a broad curved blade and a double spear point. This was the arm with which much slaughter was done in the Peninsular campaigns and at Waterloo, and made the British Light Cavalry an opponent to be feared. In 1829, a new sword was issued and continued in light cavalry service for 24 years and was only replaced in 1853 when a decision was taken to treat all troopers alike. Household Cavalry troopers carried the 1796 heavy cavalry trooper's sword until just before Victoria's accession, then heavy cavalry were issued with a sword with a blade 36 inches long, slightly curved and tapered to a sharp point. It had a steel hilt and

a bowl-shell guard lined inside with leather, which also covered the grip.

During this period, the cavalry recruit was taught to draw, carry and slope his sword and to painfully acquire the swordsman's essential suppleness of wrist and shoulder. He learned to control his weapon in attack and defence so that he applied the edge of his blade at the correct angle and prevented it from turning in his hand. He was taught the six offensive cuts, diagonals down and up, horizontal right and left, as first devised by Major Le Marchant and published in the *Rules and Regulations for the Sword Exercise of the Cavalry of 1796* (later increased to seven cuts). These cuts were complemented by seven defensive guards, designed to protect both horse and rider. Then came the Point, or Thrust, given with the nails up or down, and the Parry, a circular motion of the blade. All these movements were first carried out on foot, and repeated on horseback, with the reins gathered in the bridle hand.

The Sword, Cavalry, Pattern –/53 was the first of the weapons that were to be issued for use by all branches of the cavalry. It was primarily a thrusting weapon but the design allowed for cutting as a secondary function. The blade was straight, 36 inches in length with a guard consisting of three bars of cast-iron with a short quillon on the opposite side of the sword. As with the most new weapons of the period, issue was extended over a long time and there is no record of its use in

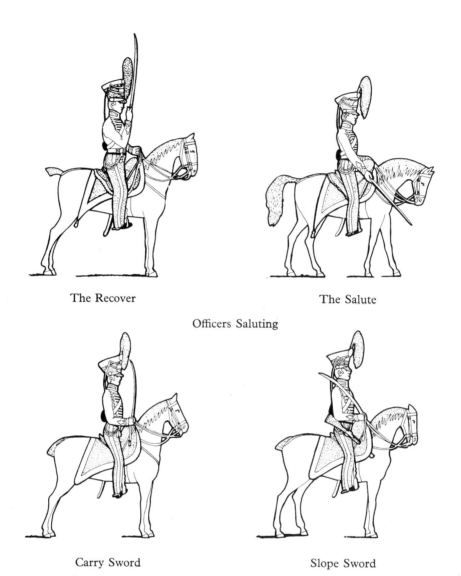

The Recover

The Salute

Officers Saluting

Carry Sword

Slope Sword

Fig. 34. Cavalry drill movements. (From Illustrations of the Field Movements of Cavalry, *by Captain Bamford, 1824.*)

either the Crimean War or the Indian Mutiny. It was carried in a steel scabbard with rings at the mouthpiece and 8 inches below it, to allow for carriage from slings.

Louis Nolan frequently denounced the steel scabbard:

'. . . the rattling, announced the cavalry's approach a mile off, and wooden scabbards would remove the necessity of wrapping the present scabbards in straw or hay'.

During the 2nd Afghan War of 1879, the 15th Hussars nearly lost the element of surprise during an attack through the rattle of sabres being drawn from steel scabbards and were themselves nearly caught unawares by Afghan horsemen who sheathed their tulwars in wooden cases. The scabbard for the 1882 sword was a slight improvement on the previous one, having fixed loops in place of rings, thus obviating some of the rattling, and was lined throughout with wax-impregnated wood; whether these two changes were as a result of Nolan's book it is hard to say.

The guard, with cast-iron bars, of the 1853 sword was replaced in 1864 by the bowl-shell guard because the cast-iron bars were often broken in action and gave little protection to the hand. At the same time the blade was shortened by an inch to 35 inches

The Charge

Preparing to Dismount

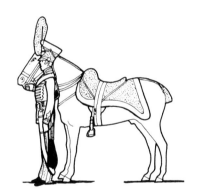

Standing to Horse, Preparatory to
Mounting and after having Dismounted

Preparing to Mount

and was curved slightly to improve the cutting edge. Although it had long been known that the inside edge of the guard was both uncomfortable to wear and damaging to the uniform, it was not until 1882 that the '64 sword was withdrawn and replaced with a weapon that had a guard with the edges of the bowl rolled over and lapped down. At the same time the blade was changed and swords of two different lengths were available, the Pattern –/82 Long, with a blade length of 35⅝th inches and the Pattern –/82 Short, having a blade of 33 inches. There is no explanation of why there should have been two lengths of sword unless it was because there were tall and short troopers!

After a cavalry encounter during the 2nd Afghan War of 1879, the 15th Hussars complained bitterly about 'wretched regulation swords which, as usual, would not cut'. After the engagement it was discovered that every single enemy horseman slain or disabled had been put out by the point alone. It was a known fault of British swords since the Heavy Cavalry in the Peninsula had only bruised or contused their French opponents and Sergeant Forbes-Mitchell (in his *Reminiscences of the Great Mutiny*) refers to the same situation in the Crimea:

'. . . it was the same in the Balaclava charge, both with the Heavy, and the Light Brigade. Their swords were too straight, and so blunt that they would not cut through the thick coats and sheepskin caps of the

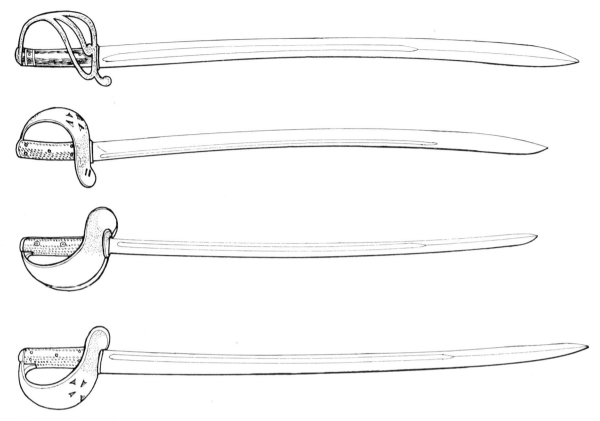

Fig. 35. Cavalry other ranks swords. From top to bottom: *1853 Pattern; 1864 Pattern; 1899 Pattern and 1885 Pattern.*

Fig. 36. British cavalry engaged in hand-to-hand fighting with natives during the Kaffir war of 1852.

Russians, so that many of our men struck with the hilts at the faces of the enemy as being more effective than attempting to cut with their blunt blades.'

The Egyptian Campaign of 1882–85 brought these failings before the public when the Press reported at considerable length on the inadequacies of the '64 and '82 pattern swords. Finally in 1884, Parliament ordered the War Office to set up a Select Committee to study the evidence of bent and broken blades, frail and unserviceable guards and grave lack of replacement stocks. Tests carried out at Aldershot in 1885 led to newspaper headlines such as 'Swords that break in action' and 'Useless swords for British soldiers.' It was revealed that 50 per cent. of the swords of the 2nd Dragoons, who were under orders for foreign service were unserviceable. The fact emerged that some British manufacturers were sub-contracting the forging of blades to German firms at Solingen and, although the blades were probably in good condition when they left Germany, bad shipping and poor storage in Britain led to the blades having to be reground before they could be assembled to the hilts. As the majority of German blades were case-hardened this regrinding weakened the structure of the metal and faulty weapons resulted.

As an interim measure, the Committee recommended that the 1882 pattern sword be modified by the adoption of a standard blade 34½ inches long; the guard should have a hand-stop fitted between the top of the grip and the knuckle-guard, and the scabbard rings should be one each side of the mouthpiece so that it could be carried strapped to the saddle. This became the Sword, Cavalry, Pattern –/85. In 1889, a further modification increased the weight of the sword by 3½ oz. so considerably affecting the point of balance of the sword, detracting from the way it could be swung in the cutting role, and adding to the strain on the trooper's wrist if held for a long time in the thrusting position. In 1890, the Sword, Cavalry, Pattern '90 was introduced, to be most unhappily received by the troopers who recognized it as yet another modification of the original sword of –/64, –/82, –/85 and –/89, and the only part affected, was once again, the blade. This retained its previous length and breadth but was of much thinner section and had a flat back, resulting in the loss of 3 oz. of the 3½ oz. it had gained the year before.

Kitchener's Omdurman Campaign of 1896–98 produced the usual spate of newspaper reports on the deficiencies in quality of the soldier's arms and equipment. The *Daily Mail* and the *Daily Telegraph* both reported the incident of a lieutenant of the Hussars whose sword had bent double against the mail-clad body of a Dervish. The outcry that arose resulted in yet another new cavalry sword, the Sword, Cavalry, Pattern –/99 – an unpopular and inadequate weapon possessing all the faults of the previous five weapons plus some more of its own. The blade was shortened to 33½ inches and the bowl considerably increased in size which necessitated the grip being lengthened from 5⅜ to 6⅜ inches, so causing the user's hand to slide up and down in an uncomfortable and inefficient manner. The bowl itself was fragile and would bend or collapse under even minor strain.

The cavalry regiments which went out to South Africa at the start of the Boer War were armed with either the 1885 or the 1890 pattern of sword but later units were issued with the thoroughly disliked 1899 model. It was not until after the Boer War, when the sword universally worn by cavalry had proved to be quite useless in action, that a really first-rate weapon was designed and made in quantity.

During the nineteenth century hardly any soldier except an infantry private could escape having to carry a sword of one pattern or another. In the British Army, Artillerymen, Engineers, Bandsmen, Pioneers and even army hospital corps troops wore them. In the Horse Artillery the private soldier was armed as for light cavalry, following all the changes until 1864 when the War Office allowed them to retain the 1853 three-bar hilt. By 1890 they were equipped with the Sword, Cavalry, Pattern –/85. From their early days as the Corps of Royal Waggoners, the private soldiers of the Army Service Corps carried light cavalry swords, except for a period from 1855–75 when they wore what John Wilkinson Latham describes as a 'Romanesque-style hanger'.* The Royal Army Veterinary Corps, both officers and other ranks, were treated as cavalry in all regulations pertaining to weapons, as were all ranks of the Military Mounted police.

A colourful adjunct to the establishment of foot regiments were the Pioneers, traditionally bearded and bearing an assortment of tools such as axes, billhooks, pick-axes and shovels. Prior to 1831, as a sidearm they carried the infantry hanger but at that time they were ordered the special Pioneers' sword. The main feature of this weapon was its broad sawbacked blade with a false edge on the last 8 inches of the back which could be used as an axe, in an emergency. This weapon had a brass stirrup hilt with a lion-head backpiece; the grip was of two brass

---

* *British Cut and Thrust Weapons*, John Wilkinson-Latham, 1971.

Fig. 39. Above: *The charge of the Heavy Brigade at Balaclava. (Coloured lithograph after William Simpson.)*

Fig. 37. Left above: *British hussars sabring the Russian gunners at Balaclava, 1854. (Coloured lithograph by A. Adam.)*

Fig. 38. Left below: *Lord Cardigan at the head of the Light Brigade during their celebrated charge at Balaclava. (Painting by T. Jones Barker.)*

pieces, indented to form finger holds. The slightly curved blade was housed in a black leather scabbard with brass top and bottom mounts, the top mount bearing a stud for suspension from a frog.

There were regimental variations to this pattern, the 52nd Foot, for instance, carrying a straight-bladed, saw-backed sword styled on the Roman gladius, having a brass-tapered grip surmounted by a lion's head and bearing the figure 52 and the badge of bugle-horn, stringed.

1856 saw the issue of a new Pioneers' sword having a straight saw-backed blade 20½ inches long and a stirrup hilt. The grip consisted of two brass sides riveted to the tang. The scabbard was of black leather with two brass mounts and was carried suspended from a frog.

Originally bandsmen were paid and equipped from the Regimental 'Music' fund to which all officers subscribed, so that regiments vied with each other in the diversity and splendour of the uniforms and equipment of their musicians. In 1824, bandsmen were mustered as soldiers and drew the pay of their equivalent rank in the fighting companies. A Royal Warrant of 1781 decreed that 'the drums and fifes' should carry a short sword, probably one of the infantry hangers of the period. From about 1850, bandsmen carried a sword with a solid cast brass hilt except for Rifle regiments when it was steel; it was emblazoned with the royal cypher for foot regiments and with the bugle-horn for light infantry. Of the regiments of Foot guards, only the Grenadiers appear to have had a distinctive badge in place of the royal cypher: a grenade surmounting a posy of roses, thistles and shamrock. The blade of this weapon was either straight or curved. A

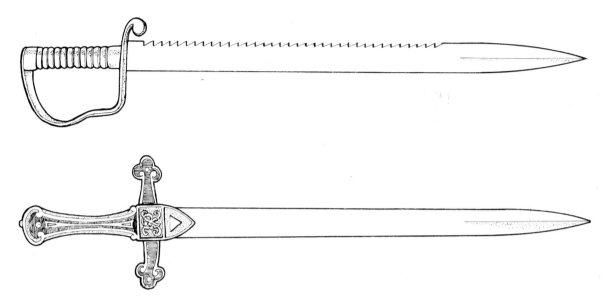

Fig. 40. Above: *Pioneer's sword, 1856–1903.* Below: *Drummer's sword, 1895.*

similar sword, but slightly lighter, was issued to buglers.

Towards the end of the nineteenth century, in the late 1890s, Line regiment bandsmen were issued with the 'Sword, drummers, Mark II and buglers, line regiments, brass with buff piece' and a black leather scabbard with two brass mounts, suspended from a white buckskin frog. Their counterparts in the rifle regiments had the same sword with a steel hilt and steel mounts on the scabbard.

At about the time of the Boer War, Regimental bands ceased to parade as such in the actual battle area and instead became stretcher-bearers, except for the buglers who were retained to play those calls necessary for the functioning of the regiment when in action.

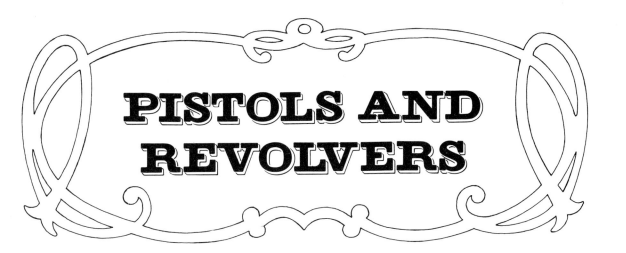

PISTOLS AND REVOLVERS

Largely because their actions were so defective in design and workmanship, revolvers were unreliable and frequently misfired so that, before 1851, they were regarded with considerable suspicion in the British Army. The authorities, always reluctant to introduce any new weapon for the rank and file, found themselves on this occasion supported by well-founded practical and technical considerations so that the revolver was ignored or condemned by the Army and Navy as an unreliable and newfangled affair. Demonstrations at the Great Exhibition of 1851 of his revolving pistol by American Colonel Sam Colt caused a partial change in the attitude of the military. In 1854 the Government set up a Select Committee on Small Arms and tests were carried out at Woolwich Arsenal to assess the relative merits of the American Colt and the British Adams revolvers. Although there was little to choose between both weapons, the Select Committee preferred the Adams, nevertheless the War Office purchased 14,000 Colts in the following year, most being issued to the Navy. In 1855 the Adams revolver was improved so that it could be used either for single or double action and, as it embodied the advantages of both the Colt and the original Adams this pattern in two different calibres .50 and .45 inches – was purchased for the Army. Less accurate than the Colt at longer ranges, the .50 Beaumont–Adams had 'the force of a steam-hammer' and could stop anything on legs.

Experiences in the field during the Crimean War and the Sepoy Mutiny also confirmed the superiority of the Adams revolvers for British military use. In the fighting which typified those conflicts, everything depended upon speed and stopping power so that the long-range accuracy of the Colt was of little value when the enemy closed in and fought hand-to-hand. Two incidents illustrate the situation. From the Crimea, J. C. Crosse of the 88th Regiment wrote to Adams:

'I had one of your largest-sized Revolver Pistols at the bloody battle of Inkerman, and by some chance got surrounded by Russians. I then found the advantages of your pistol over that of Colonel Colt's, for had I to cock before each shot I should have lost my life. I should not have had time to cock, as they were too close to me, being only a few yards from me: so close that I was bayonetted through the thigh immediately after shooting the fourth man.'

Speaking of the Sepoy Mutiny in India, Lieutenant-Colonel G. V. Fosbery noted the need for stopping power:

'An officer, who especially prided himself on his pistol-shooting, was attacked by a stalwart mutineer armed with a heavy sword. The officer, unfortunately for himself, carried a Colt's Navy pistol, which, as you may remember, was of small calibre (.36), and fired a sharp-pointed bullet of sixty to the pound and a heavy charge of powder, its range being at least 600 yards, as I have

Fig. 41. Lieutenants T. Melville and N. J. A. Coghill attempting to save the Queen's colour of the 24th Regiment at Isandhlwana, 22 January 1879. They were both killed and were posthumously awarded the Victoria Cross.

frequently proved. This he proceeded to empty into the sepoy as he advanced, but, having done so, he waited just one second too long to see the effect of his shooting, and was cloven to the teeth by his antagonist, who then dropped down and died beside him. My informant, who witnessed the affair, told me that five out of the six bullets had struck the sepoy close together in the chest, and had all passed through him and out of his back.'

In view of these and similar experiences,

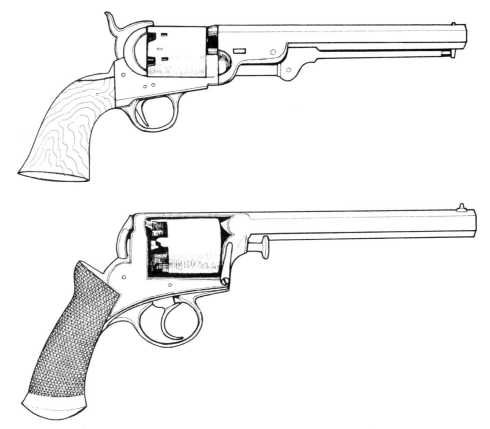

Fig. 42. Above: *Colt's Navy revolver.* Below: *Robert Adam's revolver, 1851.*

the British Government adopted the Beaumont–Adams as its official revolver. The Crimean War and the Indian Mutiny caused revolvers to become well established in the British Army particularly as officers weapons.

Both the Adams and the Colt revolvers were muzzle-loaders but from the early 1860s there was a gradual change to breech-loading. Perhaps the first breech-loading revolver was that made by William Tranter in 1863 – a .44 calibre 'police' revolver using the rim-fire cartridge popular in the United States. Those purchased for the Army are probably the only rim-fire weapons ever issued to the British Army. Tranter's 'Army' revolver, later adopted in limited quantities by the Government, used a centre-fire cartridge and all succeeding Service arms had centre fire cartridges.

In about 1880 a revolver for military use was designed and produced at the Enfield

Small Arms factory and, although not particularly good, the Enfield became the official pattern for both the Army and the Navy, becoming the first revolver to be on general issue to the rank and file of the cavalry. Of the two patterns, Mark I of 1880 had a calibre of .422 inch and the Mark II of 1882 .476 inches, the larger calibre, which was introduced as the .422 bullet had insufficient weight to stop a charging man at short range. Against tribesmen on the North-West Frontier officers armed themselves privately with more effective arms such as the .476 Enfield that fired a much heavier bullet.

The most famous of all British Army revolvers is the Webley – which holds the distinction of being the oldest pattern of British military firearm still in production in Great Britain and probably in the world. The Ordnance Board accepted Webley's Mark I in 1887 and over the succeeding seventeen years there were only a few minor

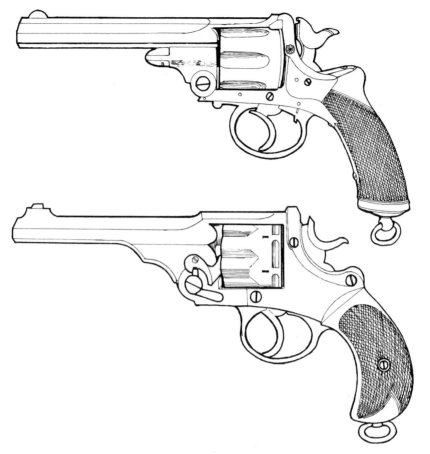

Fig. 43. Above: *Tranter's Army revolver, 1879.* Below: *Webley Army revolver, 1892 model.*

modifications. In 1877 a .38 calibre double-action lock, break-open revolver with a barrel latch and a self-ejection system was introduced under the name of the Webley-Pryse. Later a .45 Army pattern was produced – this weapon was the forerunner of Webley's Army revolvers with its main features embodied in the first of them. In 1882 Webley constructed his first break-open action revolver with a simultaneous self-ejection system, followed in 1886 by Webley's .45 Mark I which was virtually the

1882 revolver with some standardization of parts. Submitted to the Government and thoroughly tested by the Board of Ordnance it was accepted as the official revolver for the Army and 10,000 were ordered. The Mark IV Webley, produced just before the Boer War, was a standard revolver issued to the troops for the campaigns in South Africa. With two different lengths of barrel – 4 inches and 6 inches – the Mark IV was manufactured until 1914.

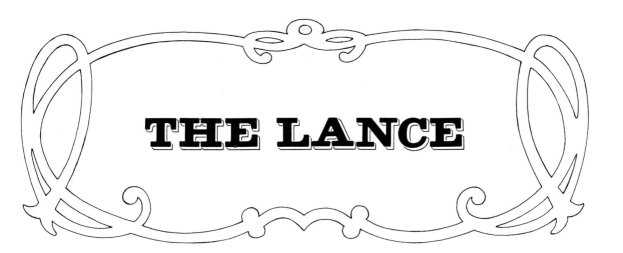

THE LANCE

The lance was one of the prime weapons of horsemen from the time when stirrups were first used and, for over one hundred years in the British Army, was considered second only to the sword as the cavalryman's weapon *par excellence*. The way in which Napoleon used regiments of Polish lancers had such an effect on British military thinking of the day that in 1816 the 9th, 12th, 16th and 23rd Light Dragoons were equipped with 16 feet lances as an experiment. Considered successful, the experiment became reality later in 1816 when the 12th took the title 'Lancers', the 16th following suit in 1817 and the 9th in 1830. In practice the 16 feet long lance proved unwieldy and the committee convened to discuss the matter decided upon a 9 feet long weapon which, plus or minus a few inches, remained its permanent length.

Captain Louis Nolan, the mid-nineteenth-century cavalry authority, wrote:

'The lancer's pennons attract the fire of artillery. . . . If lances be such good weapons, surely those who wield them ought to acquire great confidence in them, whereas it is well known that, in battle, lancers generally throw them away and take to their swords.'

This may well have been right because a lancer at the stand-still had no effective power whatsoever and it was therefore necessary for them to retain the sword for use on sentry and picquet duties and in the mêlée. Admitting that the lance instilled a sense of fear in an opponent, particularly if he was a young inexperienced soldier or a native, Nolan believed the sword to be the true cavalry weapon and thought the lance a poor substitute, useless in a mêlée and lacking penetrative power unless backed by a charge. Of course he was correct in this because the lance was only a killer when used at the gallop or at least a fast canter. Speed was essential in driving a lance home and then only if the lancer was braced in the saddle and thereby used the full weight and power of the horse in making the point.

To be used effectively, the lance had to be wielded by very well-trained troopers who, in the middle of the nineteenth century, learned the three 'Pimlico' Divisions on much the same principles as originally taught in 1816. These Divisions had been extended to six by Lieutenant-Colonel R. H. de Montmorency of the 13th Light Dragoons who had closely studied the exercises of the Polish Lancers while a prisoner of war. The first two Divisions consisted of guards against cavalry and infantry; the third taught the waves and points, the round parry and the 'St George'. The last was known also to the swordsmen as the Head Protect, with the blade held horizontally across the head with the edge upward. The lancer achieved the same object by spinning the lance horizontally above his head with the arm extended.

Lance poles (shafts) were originally of ash, impregnated with oil to retain suppleness

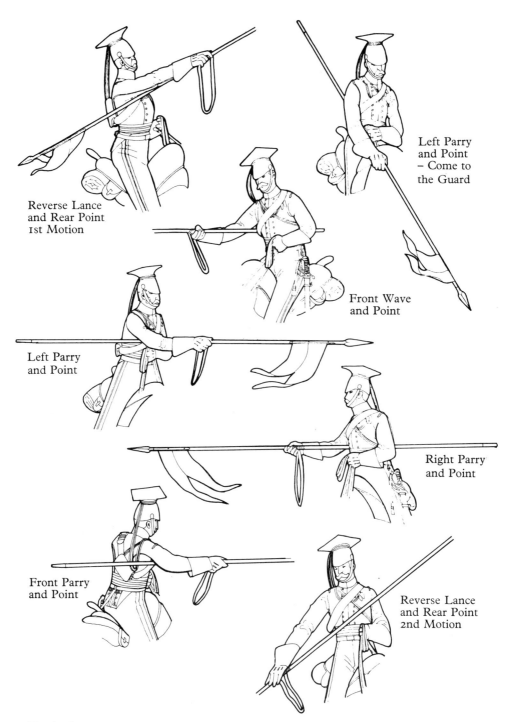

Reverse Lance
and Rear Point
1st Motion

Left Parry
and Point
– Come to
the Guard

Front Wave
and Point

Left Parry
and Point

Right Parry
and Point

Front Parry
and Point

Reverse Lance
and Rear Point
2nd Motion

Fig. 44. Typical movements from the Lance Exercise, c. 1850.

and to prevent breakage because of dryness. Unfortunately, this wood tended to warp, especially in hot climates or when stored in a warm, dry atmosphere. In 1836, because of this, male bamboo was adopted as it was solid wood right through but it had to be carefully inspected and tested to detect the ravages of boring insects in the bamboo forests of India and because of the ease with which contractors could plug and disguise the bore holes. In 1885 a return was made to ash because bamboo could only be harvested at certain seasons and was difficult to acquire but it still remained the preferred material and was used when available.

The head of the early lances had long languets that stretched down to be either pinned, screwed or rivetted to the shaft, and the 1816 model had three securing bands around both the shaft and languets. The long-serving 1868 model head had no languets and was socketed direct on to the shaft where it was held by shellac. Blade shapes varied from broad leaf to spear point and earlier models had cutting edges as well as sharp points.

During the Egyptian Campaign of 1884–85 the Arabs lay in the scrub waiting for the cavalry to come on, leaping up as the charge passed over them, attempting to hamstring the horses and throwing boomerangs of mimosa wood at their legs. Realizing that it was almost impossible for the Hussars to reach the crouching or lying Arabs with their sabres and that only lances could adequately do this job, General Stewart, after the Battle of El Teb, adapted Arab spears by weighting the heads with a roll of iron and armed his Hussars with them.

Lance pennons were small flags fastened just below the steel tip and denoted the national colours, being red and white in the British Army. After the Battle of Aliwal in 1846, the 16th Lancers paraded with their lance pennons so encrusted with dried blood that they appeared to be starched and corrugated, leading to a regimental tradition that the 16th Lancers should always parade with crimped lance pennons.

Except for odd instances such as at Elandslaagte where Lancers rode down the Boers, one young Afrikaaner receiving sixteen lance wounds, the Boer War saw the end of the lance as a practical weapon of war. Nevertheless the lance continued to be carried until 1903 when it was abolished as a war weapon only to be readopted in 1909 and carried throughout World War I. The cavalry tradition died hard in the War Office who had not noticed that Mauser rifles in practised Boer hands had decimated squadrons of Lancers before they could get to a range where their weapons would either be effectual or even intimidating. However, the rifles, machine-guns, barbed wire and artillery of 1914–18 taught an unmistakable lesson and the lance finally disappeared from the field of battle.

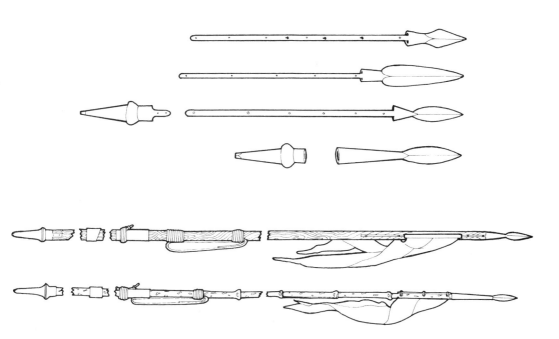

Fig. 45. From top to bottom: *Lance head, 1840; lance head, 1846; lance head and shoe, 1860; lance head and shoe, 1868; ash lance with pennon; bamboo lance with pennon.*

Fig. 46. The charge of the 16th (Queen's Own) Lancers at Aliwal, 28 January 1846. (Coloured lithograph by Harris after Martens.)

Fig. 47. The charge of the 21st (Empress of India's) Lancers at Omdurman.

Fig. 48. 'A chip off the old block.' An episode during the charge of the 5th (Royal Irish) Lancers at Elandslaagte, one of the opening battles of the South African war, 21 October 1899.

MACHINE-GUNS

Throughout the history of warfare efforts had been made to increase fire-power while reducing manpower by using a multi-firing device. The development of such a 'machine' gun was greatly hampered until the invention of metal cartridges then, as always, came a flood of such weapons. The first effective machine-gun to be designed was that of Dr Richard Gatling, an American who patented it in 1862 – just in time for minor use in the American Civil War. At Shoeburyness in August/September, 1870, the British Government tested a new and improved prototype Gatling in calibres .42; .65 and 1 inch together with the new French Montigny mitrailleuse. It was recommended that the Gatling gun be adopted and in 1871 it began to come into service.

The Gatling gun consisted of a number of very simple breech-loading rifled barrels grouped and revolving about a shaft to which they were parallel, with the re-loading and ejecting mechanism behind. The magazine was a hopper above the gun, from which the cartridges dropped by a gravity feed. The mechanism was hand operated: the gunner turned the crank handle at the side, rotating the barrels, each firing in succession. Each barrel was fired only once in a revolution but as many shots were delivered during that time as there were barrels, so that the ten-barrel Gatling gun fired ten times in one revolution of the group of barrels. The working of the gun was simple – a man placed one end of a feed case of car-

tridges in the hopper at the top of the gun while another man turned the crank wheel which revolved the gun barrels. Most popular of the various models was the ten-barrelled version, with a calibre of .45 inches and, using an improved cartridge feed, it could fire more than 600 rounds a minute. The heavy bullet, the high rate of concentrated fire plus its built-in psychological 'terror' factor, made it an ideal weapon for the Colonial Wars of the later nineteenth century.

In 1873 Sir Garnet Wolseley led an expedition against the Ashantis of West Africa and the military correspondent of *The Times* recorded on 6 October of that year that he was including a number of Gatling guns in his armaments. Actually only two of these guns went out from England shipped to West Africa by mail packet on 30 July 1873, together with 10,000 rounds of ammunition for each. Captain Rait marched from Cape Coast on the Gulf of Guinea in November 1873 taking with him the two Gatlings in addition to other artillery. After some transport difficulties one of the Gatlings arrived at the base at Prahsu. Here it was demonstrated to a group of Ashanti envoys bearing peace proposals from Kofi Karikari (King Kofi). Reports indicate that the demonstration had such remarkable results so that one of the envoys actually committed suicide! The Army and Navy Journal of the day said:

'We are not surprised that the Ashantees

58

Fig. 49. A Gatling gun in Zululand 1879.

were awe-struck before the power of the Gatling gun. It is easy to understand that it is a weapon which is specially adapted to terrify a barbarous or semi-civilized foe. The Ashantee correspondent of the *New York Herald* says that the reputation of the Gatling is now spread throughout Ashantee. "It is a terrible gun which shoots all day. Nothing could stand before it, the water of the Prah ran back affrighted." The effect of this,' remarks the writer, 'combined with many other things, has been to induce the King and his Council to deliberate and reflect on the possibility of peace.'

Of the two Gatling guns sent out from England to the Ashanti War, only one saw service when it was taken no further than the banks of the frontier River Prah where it was positioned to cope with an attack which never came. However its effective demonstration for the benefit of the Ashanti envoys would indicate that it served well as a weapon of psychological warfare.

The Royal Navy appreciated the worth of these early machine-guns before the Army. Small rapid vessels designed to carry the increasingly effective torpedo could not be effectively engaged by the heavy guns of the warships and the Gatling gun seemed to be the rapid-fire weapon that was required.

The Zulu War was the first important land operation in which Gatling guns were employed by the British Army, when they were handled by sailors of the Naval Landing Parties. Contemporary press reports indicate that the new weapon had caught the fancy of the war correspondents.

'The Gatling guns, landed with the naval contingent from the Active and Tenedos, have astonished the Zulus, who have been trying an engagement with our blue jackets. They found the fire much too hot, and the naval force has had the satisfaction of carrying more than one contested position. It is a pity that Gatlings are not more plentiful with Lord Chelmsford's army. The naval brigade have got some, but the artillery have none. If there had been a couple of Gatlings with the force annihilated the other day, the result of the fight might have been different, for Gatlings are the best of all engines of war to deal with the rush of a dense crowd.'

(*Army and Navy Gazette*, London, 22 February 1879.)

At Ginginhlovo the Gatling guns were highly effective at 1,000 yards and at

Fig. 50. 'The Naval Brigade with Gatling and Gardner guns hard at it' at the battle of El Teb, 1884. (From the Illustrated London News.)

Kambula, where they caught the Zulus, in the open, great execution was done.

'When all was over, and we counted the dead, there lay, within a radius of 500 yards, 473 Zulus. They lay in groups in some places, of fourteen to thirty dead, mowed down by the fire of the Gatling, which tells upon them more than the fire of the rifles.'

London Standard, 7 May 1879.

The Gatling gun taken to Zululand was much more simple in construction, lighter in weight and rapid in fire than that which had struck terror into the hearts of the Ashanti envoys. Instead of the old drum feeder which was fed into the side of the gun, a new upright case holding forty cartridges enabled sixty rounds a minute to be fired and the crank handle by which it was worked was now only 7 inches long. Four revolutions emptied a feeder which was instantly replaced by one of the servers of the gun.

All who witnessed the effective service that a half-battery of old-pattern Gatlings did at Ulundi in 1879, in sweeping away an encircling advance of Zulus, bore testimony to the value of this weapon. The Boxer cartridge was used in the new Gatling; but the Americans used a solid metal cartridge-case,

stamped out of the sheet. Because of the nature of their service, the small-arms ammunition used by the British soldier was subjected to more severe trials than in any other army in the world. Nevertheless, the British continued to use a compound of iron and brass, which was weak, and admitted moisture so readily that a trifling exposure ruined the powder and fulminator. This was demonstrated over and over again in Zululand during the wet season, when men carrying their cartridges in a bandolier got so many misfires that many began to lose confidence in their ammunition.

Undoubtedly the jamming of the Gatling guns was due to the use of the Boxer type of ordinary service rifle cartridges which were liable to have their base torn from the body of the case by the Gatling's extractor, leaving the metal case stuck in the chamber, so jamming it. With solid drawn cartridge cases of the American type, specially made for Gatling guns, no such difficulty was encountered.

It is worthy of note that Lord Chelmsford, despite considerable failings as a military leader, was well ahead of the military thought of his day in recognizing that the

Fig. 51. From top to bottom: *Gatling gun; Nordenfeldt gun; Maxim gun on cavalry carriage; Maxim gun on infantry carriage.*

machine-gun was an infantry and not an artillery arm. Nevertheless, it seems that he was not as favourably impressed with the new weapon as were the correspondents. Writing in 1885 in the *Journal of Royal United Services Institute*, Chelmsford said:

'On the advance of the relief of Ekowe, two Gatling guns accompanied the column, and at the battle of Ginginhlovo did considerable execution amongst the Zulus at the opening of their attack, which commenced on the north side of our position. The Zulus very soon, however, worked around to the west and south of our laager, and the Gatlings were not in action therefore for any length of time.

'At Ulundi we also had two Gatlings in the centre of the front face of our square. They jammed several times in the action, but when in work proved a very valuable addition to the strength of our defence on that flank. Machine-guns are, I consider, most valuable weapons for expeditions such as that which we had to undertake in Zululand, where the odds against us must necessarily be great, and where it is necessary to leave small detachments in charge of posts along the line of communications. The Gatlings, however, required too much care in firing, and could not be entrusted to any but skilled manipulators. If a machine-gun can be invented that may safely be entrusted to infantry soldiers to work, and could be fired very much as one grinds an organ, I am satisfied of its great value. They should, however, be considered as essentially an infantry weapon, and should be worked by infantry soldiers. So utilized, they might, I feel sure, be used most effectively not only in defence, but in covering the last stage of an infantry attack upon a position where the troops have at last to cease firing and endeavour to get home with the bayonet.'

At the bombardment of Alexandria in the summer of 1882, Gatling guns were mounted in the tops of ships in order to bring a plunging fire down on the enemy batteries but the results were disappointing, probably because of smoke from the big guns and the Gatlings themselves which obscured the view of their crews. A few days later a party of blue jackets and Marines made highly effective use of Gatling guns in the streets of Alexandria when controlling mobs of looters. In action at Chalouf and at Mahuta in 1882, the Naval Gatling guns performed most effectively as they did at Tel-el-Kebir on 12 September 1882. The *Army and Navy Gazette* described the events:

'The naval machine-gun battery, consisting of six Gatlings, manned by thirty seamen, reached the position assigned to it in the English lines on September 10th and, on Tuesday, September 12th, received orders to advance. They came within easy range of the Tel-el-Kebir earthworks, and observed guns in front, guns to the right, guns to the left, and a living line of fire above them. Nothing daunted, the order, "action-front", was given, and was taken up joyously by every gun's crew. Round whisked the Gatlings, r-r-r-r-r-rum! r-r-r-r-r-rum! that hellish noise the soldier so much detests in action, not for what it has done, so much as what it could do, rattled out. The report of the machine-guns, as they rattle away, rings out clearly on the morning air. The parapets are swept. The embrasures are literally plugged with bullets. The flashes cease to come from them. With a cheer the Blue Jackets double over the dam, and dash over the parapet, only just in time to find their enemy in full retreat. That machine-gun was too much for them. Skulking under the parapet were found a few poor devils, too frightened to retire, yet willing enough to stab a Christian, if helpless and wounded. The trenches were full of dead. But few wounded were found. Captain FitzRoy led his men most gallantly, and followed up the retreating foe until the main camp was reached. Here the halt was sounded. Admiral Sir Beauchamp Seymour and staff now came up and addressed the battery, complimenting the officers and men on their gallantry.'

As in Zululand, the Gatling guns that took part in the Egyptian and Sudanese campaigns were still being manned by sailors although in 1875 the Royal Artillery had received Gatling guns as part of their equipment, being ordered to handle them as field guns, using a limber with shafts and harness.

It was of the desert battles in the Sudan

Fig. 52. Gatling guns at Tayoong Heights, Burma, 1886.

that Sir Henry Newbolt wrote in *Vitai Lampada*:

'The sand of the desert is sodden red,
Red with the wreck of a square that broke;
The Gatling's jammed and the Colonel dead,
And the regiment blind with dust and smoke.'

Perhaps he refers to the square that gave way at Tamai where the tribesmen overran the machine-guns, although not before they had been locked by the heroic Naval Brigade, who stood by them till the last, losing three officers and many blue-jackets. On mobile carriages, Gatling guns were taken ashore by Naval brigades and there is a well-known drawing by war artist Melton Prior of them in action at the Battle of El Teb in 1884. Here, Graham's force advanced in a huge square with guns and Gatlings at the corners, cavalry and mounted infantry out all round, the transport animals in the centre. They came under heavy shrapnel fire from Krupp guns captured by Dervishes from Baker Pasha, served by impressed artillery-

men from the captured garrison of Tokar. Later two of these guns were put out of action by artillery and machine-gun fire at 900 yards. The Arabs then attacked and were turned back with considerable losses by massed fire from ten-barrelled Nordenfeldts, Gardner guns and rifles (the British infantry had sliced off the heads of the bullets but even these expanding 'dum-dums' did not always stop the natives). Colonel Burnaby picked off thirteen tribesmen with twenty-three shots from his double-barrelled twelve bore loaded with pig-shot. The whole battle was a convincing demonstration of the superiority of discipline backed by Martini rifles and machine-guns over numbers and fanatical courage. The *Daily Telegraph* wrote, 'The supremacy of the Anglo-Saxon race over the children of the desert was amply manifested.'

The Royal Navy chose the Gardner machine-gun to replace the Gatling in the mid-1870s. This gun had five barrels fitted side by side, was .45 in. in calibre and, with a portable tripod, weighed 369 lbs. The cartridges were in clips fed into the guns vertically and, like the Gatling, the gun was

Fig. 53. India, North-West Frontier, 1898. A Maxim gun at Chilas Fort.

Fig. 54. A Maxim gun detachment of the King's Royal Rifle Corps during the Chitral campaign, 1895.

operated by cranking a handle, the rate of cranking controlling the rate of fire which could be up to 120 rounds per minute with each barrel. This gun was also used by Naval brigades in the Sudan. Stewart's desert column included thirty of Beresford's Blue Jackets pulling a Gardner gun which, at Abu Klea, played a prominent part when the Arabs came down on the left rear corner with lightning speed. This was the square's most vulnerable point, where it had been bulged out by the camels as well as 'gapped' by the Gardner gun, which the Naval Brigade had run out about 20 yards outside the left rear face. Numbers of the fast-moving Arabs dropped over the last hundred yards but the number of rifles was insufficient to turn them back, and in a few seconds the left rear corner was pressed back by sheer weight of number. At this stage, the Gardner gun jammed, causing the loss of nearly half the Naval Brigade who gallantly fought around it till they were slaughtered or swept into the square by the rush of Arabs.

The Nordenfeldt four-barrelled gun, firing more than 200 1-inch calibre rounds per minute replaced both Gatling and Gardner guns in the Royal Navy from 1880 onwards. In July 1883 a five-barrelled Nordenfeldt gun mounted on an ordinary infantry carriage, was adopted as an auxiliary arm by the Central London Rangers; a detachment of ten men under Captain Armit at Dartford showed that the time taken from 'order' to 'halt', in reversing the gun, opening the limber, mounting the carriage-hopper and firing 50 rounds was only 22 seconds.

These early machine-guns were all hand-cranked but the machine-gun, invented by American Hiram Maxim, was revolutionary in that its recoil was used to load, fire and eject continuously while the trigger was held back; the cartridges were stored in a flexible belt and the gun was cooled by a water jacket round the barrel. Most successful in its trials in 1884, the Maxim's high-rate of fire was maintained at a cost of £5 per minute, which caused the King of Denmark to decide that his country could not afford it. Suitably impressed, the British Government agreed to buy if the weight could be reduced to 100 lbs

and the rate of firing increased to 400 rounds a minute so Maxim made a new model weighing only 40 lbs and firing 650 rounds a minute. Introduced into the British Army in 1891, it was issued gradually to cavalry and infantry and not to the gunners. A variety of carriages, nearly all without limbers, were introduced, those issued to cavalry being higher than the infantry type.

If it possessed the range, the Maxim had to stop man or horse for the rapidity of fire was so great that four or five bullets struck a man before he fell. The earlier Martini–Henry calibre Maxim had a large bullet, but the smoke of its black powder drew fire. The later smokeless Maxims were invaluable for the defence of the frontier posts where the ranges could be marked and ammunition stored. One of the first recorded uses of the Maxim machine-gun in action was in an expedition against the Isazai tribes on the North-West Frontier of India in 1892. At Dargai in 1897, the Gordons and the Maxim detachment supported the attack with long-range fire at about 1,100 yards, while mountain batteries kept up an accurate and well-sustained fire at 3,300 yards range. During Kitchener's Omdurman campaign a Maxim battery of four machine-guns was formed from the combined machine-gun section of the North Staffords and the Connaught Rangers to add to the fire-power of the infantry. At the actual Battle of Omdurman it was written that – 'the Maxims opened fire with tremendous effect, the attack began to thin and waver; a rigid line would gather itself up and rush on evenly, then suddenly quiver and stop; then other lines would gather themselves up again, again and yet again but, they went down and others rushed on.'

Maxim had designed a heavier machine-gun of 1.46 in. calibre known as the pom-pom that also fired an explosive shell. Because of its weight it was a carriage gun and was used extensively by the Boers against the British in South Africa during the war of 1899–1902. With only slight modifications the Maxim machine-gun, as the Vickers–Maxim and later Vickers, was used by the British Army in both world wars.

Fig. 55. Above: *Royal Horse Artillery, 1846. (Coloured lithograph after M. A. Hayes (detail).)*

Fig. 56. Below: *Royal Horse Artillery, 'Fire' (Right flank thrown back for action-right). No. 4 in a set of six coloured lithographs after G. B. Campion, c. 1846.*

ARTILLERY

During the 20 years period that followed Waterloo, neglect and apathy prevented progress so that in 1854 the British Army went into the Crimean War with cannon that had been used at Waterloo. After 1815 most of the large British Army was disbanded and the Royal Artillery and the Royal Horse Artillery were reduced to a fraction of their former size. At the same time British Artillery became more stable as the 12 pdr and the long 6 pdr guns ceased to be used as field artillery and the $4\frac{2}{5}$ and $5\frac{1}{2}$ in. howitzers were replaced in 1822 by the longer 12 and 24 pdr howitzers. British Horse Artillery troops were usually equipped with four light 6 pdr guns and two 12 pdr howitzers while the field batteries normally had four 9 pdr guns and two 24 pdr howitzers.

Following the complete breakdown of transport during the first winter of the Crimean War, the Board of Ordnance was abolished after 400 years of unbroken power and the artillery engineers came under the direct control of the War Office and the Commander-in-Chief, like the rest of the Army.

For the first half of the Victorian era, the guns used by the British Army were smooth-bore, muzzle-loaders almost exactly the same as those used at Waterloo and for more than a hundred years before that. The heavy barrel was supported on a carriage consisting of a pair of wheels and an axle-tree with the front end of a long trail permanently fixed to it. The rear end of the trail rested on the ground when the gun was in action and as the piece was fired, the backward thrust of the explosion was transmitted down the sloping trail and absorbed to some extent by the ground. Before Congreve introduced the block-trail into British service in 1792, the carriage was made very cumbersome by the long and very heavy trails which required great efforts by two men with 6-ft wooden hand spikes to move them, the laying of the piece being carried out by the 'Number One' after these two gunners had man-handled the trail. The new trail was a pole-like structure, square in section that shifted the centre of gravity further forward of the whole carriage so that one man could lift the trail off the ground with a single short hand spike. As that man could be the 'Number One' himself, he could lay the gun far more quickly and accurately than when working through two other crewmen. Another advantage lay in the carriage being able to be reversed almost on its own ground. Congreve's block-trail was in service with all British 6 and 9 pdr guns from the Peninsular War onwards and the 12 and 24 pdr howitzers had block-trails from their inception.

The performance of British smooth-bore guns was very fully recorded up to 1860 when they began to be superseded by rifled breech-loaders. Becoming after Waterloo the standard equipment of the British and Indian Horse Artilleries, the light 6 pdr gun was more constantly in action than any other British piece of artillery. With muzzle

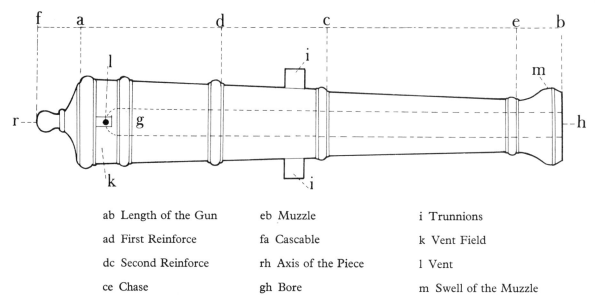

ab Length of the Gun	eb Muzzle	i Trunnions
ad First Reinforce	fa Cascable	k Vent Field
dc Second Reinforce	rh Axis of the Piece	l Vent
ce Chase	gh Bore	m Swell of the Muzzle

Fig. 57. Parts of the cannon.

velocities of between 1,500 and 1,700 feet per second, the 6 pdr (with a 1½ lb. charge) could fire roundshot as far as 1,200 yards. Backed by the 9 pdr gun, the 6 pdr was the one British light gun continually in service during the whole era of smooth-bore ordnance. The Bengal Horse Artillery took the 6 pdr gun to Afghanistan in 1839 and lost them when the troop was annihilated, firing its guns to the last man. The same battery recaptured one of those guns 40 years later at Ahmed Khel in the 2nd Afghan War. In the Sikh Wars of 1846 and 1849, the Horse Artillery galloped through a storm of roundshot to engage the heavier Sikh Artillery at caseshot range and distinguished itself at Balaclava in the Crimea when defending the redoubts on Canrobert Hill, preventing the Russian cavalry from rallying after the charge of the Heavy Brigade. In his book *Guns and Cavalry* (1896) Major E. S. May wrote:

'In the old days of roundshot and case a good Horse Artillery range was 400 yards; 200 yards was even better. The Horse Artillery guns were comparatively useless unless they gallop right into a fight, their whole energies were concentrated on getting to close quarters as soon as possible. Even on the battlefield itself they might gallop up to within a few hundred yards of a mass of infantry, unlimber and come into action without excessive loss, and then a pitiless storm of case was often more than a match for the musketry fire which clumsy flintlocks could bring to bear.'

The heavier 9 pdr gun was used by field batteries; with a 3 lb. charge it had a range of 1,400 yards. At the Alma in 1854 it was a battery of 9 pdrs that was ordered up by Lord Raglan to the commanding ridge amid the enemy's position on which he had inadvertently ridden with his staff.

It was generally accepted that light guns could be fired at the rate of eight rounds a minute with full sponging and nine without although in action a rate of fire of three rounds a minute of case and two of roundshot was more usual. This decrease in rate of fire can be laid down to delays in relaying the gun because of the clouds of smoke and to the meticulously carried out gun drills designed to prevent accidents and performed more with rhythm than speed. By far the greater time was taken 'running up' the carriage after the recoil on firing (the average recoil of a light gun was about 3½ feet) and in relaying it – it took an experienced gun detachment only about 5 seconds to sponge, load and fire a light gun.

It was probably 6 pdrs that are reported to have fired 2,613 rounds when '. . . breaking

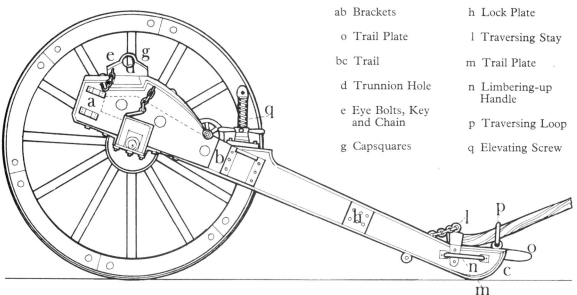

ab Brackets	h Lock Plate
o Trail Plate	l Traversing Stay
bc Trail	m Trail Plate
d Trunnion Hole	n Limbering-up Handle
e Eye Bolts, Key and Chain	p Traversing Loop
g Capsquares	q Elevating Screw

Fig. 58. Parts of the gun carriage.

the enemy centre . . . galloping to the edge of the nullah and enfilading the tribesmen . . . chasing the enemy with the cavalry and repeatedly unlimbering to fire upon the fugitives' during a punitive expedition on Shakot led by Sir Colin Campbell in 1852.

The rate of fire of a light gun in action is confirmed by two hypothetical situations set out in an 1848 Madras Artillery training manual. The first concerns an attack by cavalry on a gun position, commencing a mile away when they would trot for the first half mile, gallop for the next quarter and increase their speed to end with a charge – the whole taking about 6 minutes. During that time each gun would be expected to fire:

From 1,500 to 650 yards – 7 spherical case.
From 650 to 350 yards – 2 roundshot.
From 350 to point-blank range – 2 case-shot.

The second situation assumed an attack by infantry who took 16½ minutes to cover 1,500 yards, during which time each gun would fire:

From 1,500 to 650 yards – 19 spherical case.

From 650 to 350 yards – 7 roundshot.
From 350 to 100 yards – 8 caseshot.
From 100 yards to point-blank range – 2 caseshot.

Even if the firing was only average, the point would seem to be made that a frontal attack on a gun position was rather hazardous.

There were 18, 24 and 32 pdr guns continually in service from 1700 to 1860 when heavy artillery was primarily used for siege operations against fortresses although lighter and more mobile heavy equipment often operated as heavy field artillery because of its ability to discharge a greater weight of metal than the light equipment. Eighteen pdr guns and 8 in. howitzers were frequently used in the field during nineteenth-century wars in India, notably at Sobraon and Gujerat in the first and second Sikh Wars. It was to cover the battering train moving up from Delhi that Gough sent out Sir Harry Smith to fight the Battle of Aliwal, only for these guns to run out of ammunition before effectively destroying the Sikh defences at Sobraon in 1846. During this battle and in the second Sikh War, British 'heavies' fired effectively from ranges of 900 to 1,500 yards. The 24

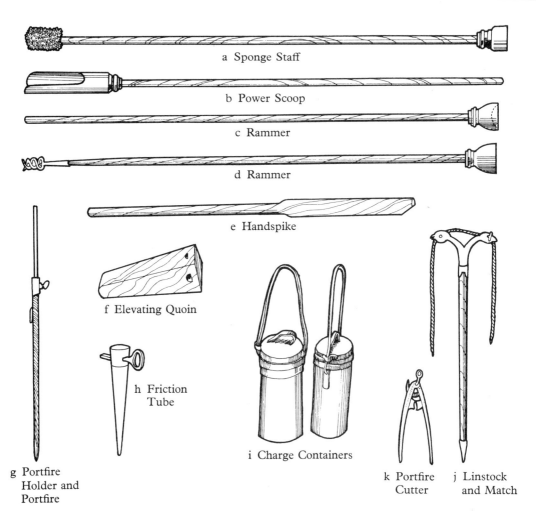

a Sponge Staff

b Power Scoop

c Rammer

d Rammer

e Handspike

f Elevating Quoin

h Friction Tube

i Charge Containers

g Portfire Holder and Portfire

k Portfire Cutter

j Linstock and Match

Fig. 59. Artillery tools.

pdr 50 cwt gun was considered to be the most efficient breaching weapon in the world and its roundshot could penetrate 12 feet of rammed earth. It was present at all the sieges in the Peninsula besides being at Delhi and Lucknow during the Indian Mutiny, when the six 24 pdr guns taken from the H.M.S. *Shannon* and mounted on land service carriages, dragged through the heat of the Indian summer by Naval ratings under Captain William Peel, played a leading part in the relief and siege of Lucknow and at Cawnpore. It is worth remembering that the 24 pdr gun had a 'behind the team' weight of 81 cwts; the 18 pdr and the 32 pdr weighed 65½ cwts and 85 cwts respectively.

The 18 pdr gun was an invaluable member of every British siege train being used to neutralize the defending guns in fortresses. Used in this manner at the siege of Delhi, the 18 pdrs destroyed the three bastions most likely to cause trouble to the attacking force. At Inkerman in November 1854, two 18 pdr guns, one drawn by a double team of horses and the other dragged uphill by the willing hands of as many men as could be gathered together, unlimbering in the open under heavy fire, the guns were steadily layed to throw their heavy 18 pdr shot into the Russian position until gun after gun was disabled. It was the turning-point of the battle as the Russian infantry and a part of their artillery support were thrown back. Also in the Crimea, 68 pdr guns manned by naval ratings were used at Sebastopol.

The 8 in. howitzer played a notable part in most of the field operations carried out in India during the nineteenth century, being

a Solid Shot attached
to wooden Sabot.

b Case, or
Canister, with
Cartridge
attached.

c Explosive and Shrapnel
Shell, 1784-1854.

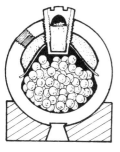

d Boxer's Diaphragm
Shrapnel Shell.

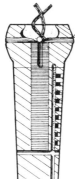

ef Boxer's Time Fuze.

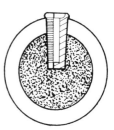

g Explosive Shell
with Boxer Fuze.

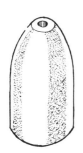

h Armstrong lead-coated
Shell, B.L., 1854.

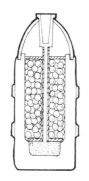

j Boxer's modified
Shrapnel, 1860-69.

k Studded Shell
(Woolwich), M.L.,
1869.

l Studded Shell
with Gas check,
1869-78.

Fig. 60. Types of artillery projectiles.

Fig. 61. The 'Grey' Battery Royal Artillery embarking for the Crimea. (Watercolour by W. Harris.)

particularly effective at Lucknow and during the siege of Delhi. Firing spherical case and common shell to a range of 1,700 yards, it was often used as heavy field artillery as an alternative to the 18 pdr gun. Two of these guns, drawn by elephants, accompanied Sir Colin Campbell at the end of 1851 when he led an expedition into the Swat Valley on the North-West Frontier of India.

At sieges such as Sebastopol in the Crimea, mortars flung their common shell or carcasses over walls and ramparts, firing from the covered positions permitted by their high trajectory. It was usually possible to select the best type for a particular operation, as they covered a wide range of calibres and weights. There were brass mortars of 10 inches, 8 inches, 5½ inches, 4⅖ inches (coehorn) with ranges of 1,300 yards, 1,600 yards, 1,000 yards and 800 yards respectively. Iron mortars of 13 inches, 10 inches and 8 inches had ranges of 2,700 yards, 2,500 yards and 1,700 yards respectively. With no heavy howitzers in the siege-train at Sebastopol, mortars played a very big part in the operations as they did during the siege of Delhi in 1857. Here, manned by native artil-

lerymen of the Bengal Horse Artillery, in the stifling heat of September days and nights the four 10 in. and six 8 in. mortars kept up a destructive fire that prevented interference with the vital breaching operations before the final assault.

From 1820 to 1860 the guns as listed in the table were in British service.

In action the solid smooth-bore gun was not easily damaged although it could be dismounted from its carriage. The most vulnerable part of the weapon was its vent and, if blocked, it was impossible to fire the piece. During an attack guns were 'spiked' by driving a metal spike down the vent so that it would be temporarily useless even if recaptured. Assaulting troops carried supplies of spikes for this purpose and sometimes parties of gunners followed up the attacking infantry to carry out a more professional job on the captured enemy guns. The normal method of unspiking a gun was to place a small charge in the bore and run a quick match down the bore from muzzle to charge. The muzzle was then blocked with shot and clods of earth; then the charge fired in the hope of blowing out the spike. If this did not

BRASS	RANGE (Yards)
Light and Medium 12 pdr	1,400
9 pdr	1,400
Long 6 pdr (doubtful if used in Crimea)	1,400
Light 6 pdr	1,200
Long 3 pdr (out of service by 1850) Light 3 pdr (also Mountain gun)	1,200

IRON	
8″ (used in siege-train in Crimea)	3,250
42 pdr (Coast Artillery)	3,100
68 pdr	3,170
12″; 10″; 8″ shell gun	3,170–3,250
32 pdr (Coast and siege artillery)	2,900
24 pdr (Most effective breaching gun in siege-train	1,900 at 5° 2,400 at 10°
18 pdr (Siege-train and heavy field battery)	1,800 at 5° 2,300 at 10°

work, the very laborious task of drilling a new vent had to be undertaken.

Both on land and sea, the second half of the nineteenth century were years of great advancement for British Services when rifled breech-loading guns discharging cylindrical projectiles replaced the old cast-iron or bronze, smooth-bore, muzzle-loading guns discharging roundshot or shell. Quite rightly it was thought that the rifling of cannon would increase their effectiveness as much as the rifling of small arms had done for the infantryman. The following table (taken from *The Story of the Gun* by Lieutenant A. W. Wilson RA, 1944, published by the Royal Artillery Institution, Woolwich) lists the principal types in the Field Army Artillery during the latter half of the nineteenth century.

From 1850 to 1900 artillery advanced to a stage where only further minor changes in design produced the guns used in World Wars I and II. The British Navy and Army began the change to iron and steel breech-loading guns in the 1850s and the Government, economy-minded as always, instructed that old guns were to be modified wherever possible so that in 1854 cast-iron, muzzle-loading smooth-bore 68 pdrs and 8 in. guns were converted into rifled ordnance on the Lancaster principle. This increased the range of these guns to 2,600 yards and a contemporary report says that it made the bombardment of Sebastopol 'A very hideous

DECADE	CATEGORY	HORSE	FIELD	MOUNTAIN	HEAVY
The 50's	S.B.	6 pr. gun	9 pr. gun	3 pr. gun	18 pr. gun
		12 pr. gun	24 pr. how.	12 pr. how.	8″ mortar
The 60's	R.B.L.	9 pr. gun	12 pr. gun	6 pr. gun	40 pr. gun
					8″ mortar
The 70's	R.M.L.	9 pr. gun	9 and 16 pr. guns	7 pr. gun	40 pr. gun
					6·3″ how.
The 80's	B.L.	*13 pr. gun	*13 pr. gun	2·5″ gun	30 pr. gun
		12 pr. gun (7 cwt)	12 pr. gun (7 cwt)		6·3″ how.
The 90's	B.L.	12 pr. gun (6 cwt)	15 pr. gun	2·5″ gun	40 pr. gun
			5″ how.		6·3″ how.

* The 13 pdr gun was in fact the R.M.L. gun introduced to stave off a reversion to breech-loading. It was superseded by the 12 pdr B.L.

thing'. Nevertheless the gun was not considered successful and its use was discontinued.

One lesson the British Army had learned in the Crimea was that the range of smooth-bore field guns was very little more than that of the infantryman's new rifle so that the artilleryman was equally as vulnerable as the infantry he was attempting to blast from the front of his position. Perhaps more than any other battle it was that of Inkerman in 1854 that showed the need for light guns with a much longer range.

Subsequently William (later Lord) Armstrong experimented with production methods so that, in July 1855, he was able to deliver to the Ordnance Select Committee a 3 pdr, his first gun, quickly followed by an 18 pdr. Armstrong's 3 pdr breech-loading rifle gun was built on the entirely new prin-

ciple of using thin wrought-iron coils or layers shrunk on to an inner tube, to give increased strength to the bore. Later rebored to a 5 pdr, the 3 pdr revealed itself in its trials as a first-class weapon with an effective range of 1,500 to 2,000 yards. In January 1859 the British Government ordered a number of field guns of various calibres from Armstrong and eventually the Horse Artillery were equipped with 9 pdrs weighing 6 cwt, the field batteries with 12 pdrs weighing 8 cwt; both with wood carriages. The guns first saw action in the British service in China in 1860, and were taken by the expedition to Bhutan in 1864. Armstrong's muzzle-loaders were well in advance of their time and are said to have been used in the British Army with very few changes as late as the Boer War. Ayoub Khan, the Afghan leader, used Armstrong guns *against*

Fig. 62. Smooth-bore field pieces. Above: *12-pdr field gun and limber.* Centre: *9-pdr field gun.* Below: *24-pdr howitzer.*

KEY

1 Gun Commander	3 Loader	5 Firer
2 Spongeman	4 Ventsman	6/7 Ammunition Servers

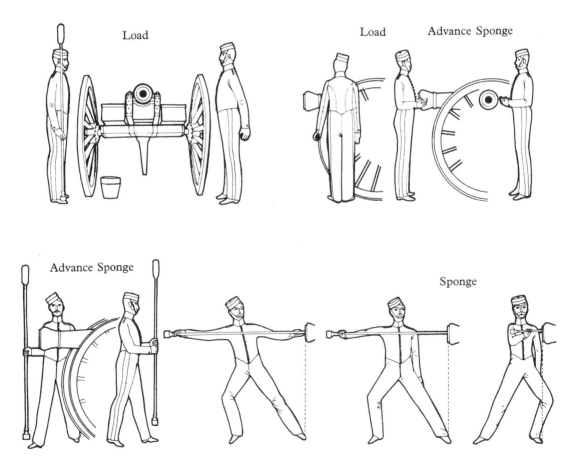

Fig. 63. Top of page: *Positions of part of a gun detachment at exercise or in action.* Below and right: *Drill movements in the service of muzzle-loading artillery, c. 1850.*

Ram Home Cartridge   Spring Rammer

Draw Rammer

Load   Ready

Ready   Fire

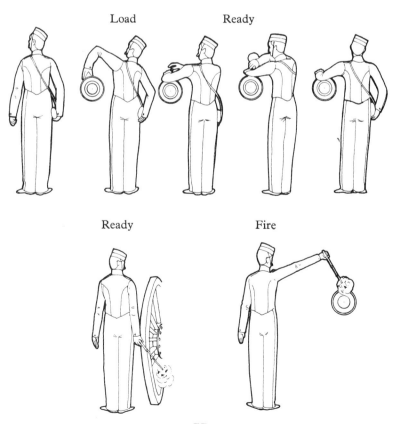

77

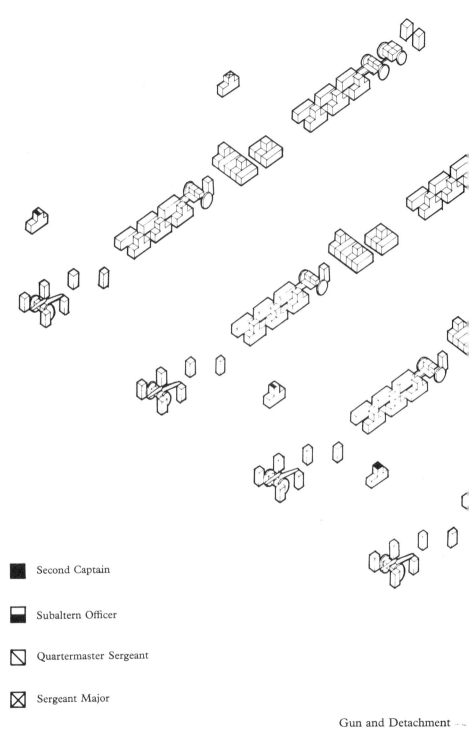

Second Captain

Subaltern Officer

Quartermaster Sergeant

Sergeant Major

Gun and Detachment

Fig. 64. The Horse Artillery Troop formed in line for Action-front, c. 1854.

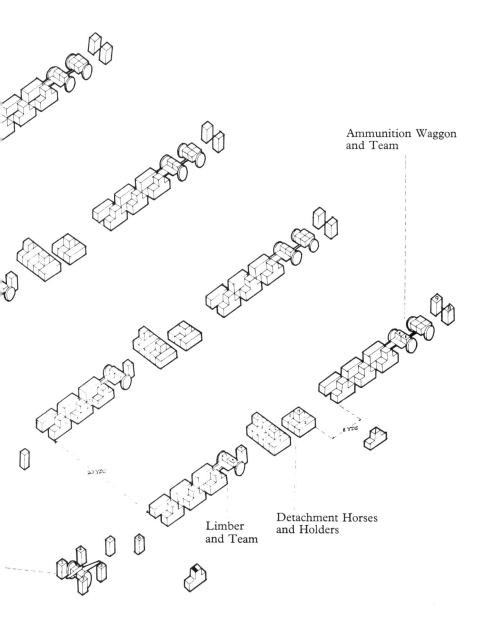

Ammunition Waggon
and Team

Limber
and Team

Detachment Horses
and Holders

79

Fig. 65. The Foot Artillery, 1846. (Coloured lithograph after M. A. Hayes (detail).)

the British force of General Roberts in front of Kandahar in 1880.

Shells fired from the Armstrong guns had fuses that allowed them to fill more than one role – the projectile could be used as canister by bursting shortly after it left the gun; as shrapnel by air burst above and in front of the target; as common shell by bursting it on impact and finally when attacking protected targets, by bursting it after it had penetrated a wall or barrier.

Armstrong made both breech- and muzzle-loading guns for the Confederacy during the American Civil War and although no rifled pieces of foreign make other than Armstrong, Whitworth and Blakeley seem to have been used in the field during that war, these guns from Britain constituted only a small part of the Confederate artillery. In many ways they were a most modern and progressive artillery, containing in embryo most of the improvements that went into the weapons of World Wars I and II. The large British guns had range, power and accuracy exceeding anything made in America where artillery was essentially no different from that used by Cromwell two centuries before. British Whitworth guns also were used by the Confederacy and held in high regard by their users as they completely outclassed all contemporary guns (except the Armstrong) for they carried three times as far as any Union field gun and were as accurate at 9,000 yards as a Napoleon field piece was at 1,000. Innumerable well-documented incidents show that professional gunners took full advantage of the good qualities of these weapons which, in range and accuracy,

Fig. 66. Royal Artillery, 10 in. howitzer and 18-pdr siege guns. No. 2 in a set of six coloured lithographs after G. B. Campion, c. 1846.

were almost as good as the artillery of World War I although their bursting charges were far less powerful. The Whitworth had the disadvantages of a tendency for the shell to jam in the bore and, at close range, the Whitworth could fire canister only with serious danger to its crew.

By 1864, perhaps because they were well in advance of their time, they had lost much of their popularity and had been replaced by the muzzle-loading, smooth-bore, bronze 12 pdr Napoleon gun. Used like a monster shot-gun with double charges of canister at close range, it was a deadly weapon that was to remain the principal artillery piece in the United States Army for almost 25 years. This type of gun was more effective at close range and was far less expensive although the rifled guns had the range and accuracy but the American Civil War was fought in such a manner as to discourage the advocates of rifled cannon and other improvements in artillery design.

The British breech-loading guns of built-up construction were capable of both accuracy and penetration but were undervalued probably because they were used ahead of their time. The extremely long ranges attainable with them could not be displayed to full advantage because of contemporary faults in the technique of gunnery and communications. For example, in trials the $1\frac{1}{2}$ pdr Whitworth gun threw its projectile 9,500 yards but could not be tested for accuracy at that range because the ground was too short! Tests were conducted on 'a line of sight' basis because accurate methods of indirect fire were not yet in use. Then it had to be faced that production facilities were inadequate to construct these weapons in any quantities – even in such experienced firms as Armstrong and Whitworth the manufacturing methods lagged behind the work of the scientist and the inventor.

Armstrong guns featured in a relatively unique situation during the Maori Wars in New Zealand when, in 1864, the Naval Brigade brought ashore an Armstrong 110 pdr gun, the heaviest gun in the Service and almost certainly the heaviest gun ever used on shore against natives. In addition the British force had two 40 pdr Armstrongs; two 24 pdr howitzers and eight mortars. When the sun rose, the guns, including the big 110 pdr, opened fire, sending their shells roaring through the air. Over the pah a red flag waved on a tall mast, from the batteries it seemed to be in the centre of the pah and most of the gunners took it for their mark in laying their pieces; it was later discovered that the flagstaff stood further off just behind the rearward stockade so that for the first two hours many of the shells passed harmlessly over the Maori position. In an effort to make a breach in the parapet, the guns were directed on the left angle of the fort. Every now and then a brave Maori would creep up to the crumbling mound and shovel a few spadefuls of earth into the gap and slip back again; once a native actually succeeded in hanging a blanket across the breach to conceal the movements of those bringing up repairing materials. The place was completely surrounded with thirteen guns and mortars blazing away at it; the big Armstrong gun fired no less than a hundred 110 lb. shells before it ceased firing at three o'clock for want of ammunition. It was later discovered that the Maoris, crouching in their hollowed-out shelters in the trenches, suffered very few casualties, being greatly encouraged by the realization that even though the shells made a terrible noise they killed or wounded very few men.

Although he constructed breech-loaders, Whitworth believed that muzzle-loaders were cheaper, safer and just as efficient so he continued working on muzzle-loading guns. In 1863, official trials were begun in Britain and the most important weapons in the trial were Whitworth's new 12 and 70 pdr muzzle-loaders and Armstrong breech-loaders of the same size together with two Armstrong muzzle-loaders. In August 1865, the Committee reported on both field and heavy guns:

'The many-groove system of rifling with its lead-coated projectiles and complicated breech-loading arrangements (i.e. Armstrong's guns) is far inferior for the general purpose of war, to both the muzzle-loading system (Whitworth's and Armstrong's) and has the disadvantage of being more expensive both in original cost and ammunition. Muzzle-loading guns are far superior to breech-loaders in simplicity of construction and efficiency in this respect for active service; they can be loaded and worked with perfect ease and abundant rapidity.'

The Committee also decided that

Armstrong's steel barrel with superimposed hoops of wrought iron was a safer method of construction than Whitworth's steel only method and, although the former system was the best method of construction, it was expensive. (By 1867, the Government's gun factories at Woolwich had devised an alternative way of building up a gun that soon became fairly standardized.) The report encouraged the ruling that Ordnance of the heavier type should be muzzle-loading and rifled in the French pattern. This method had the advantage of allowing the projectile to be used with muzzle-loading guns whereas Armstrong's lead-coated shell could only be used with breech-loaders. The British Government experimented with the French method and found it so satisfactory that even as they equipped the Horse and Field Artillery with Armstrong's new 9 and 12 pdr breech-loading guns they were planning wrought-iron built-up muzzle-loading rifled guns of 40 lbs and more. Supporters of the muzzle-loader were delighted when it was found that the Armstrong 7-in. rifled breech-loader was not a success and that even on the lighter pieces the breech action was not particularly effective.

Heated arguments on the merits of breech- and muzzle-loading guns were frequent as soldiers and experts 'aired their views'. Sir Andrew Noble, an advocate of rifled guns, was trying on one occasion to convince a senior artillery officer that the rifled guns were more accurate than the smooth-bores and, to support his case, he drew a diagram showing that shot from a rifled gun fell into a much smaller area than those of the smooth-bore. The eminent gunner was not shaken: 'That only proves what I have always maintained that our smooth-bore is the best in the world. With your new-fangled gun firing at me I've only to keep outside that small area and I shan't be touched but with the smooth-bore firing at me I'm not safe anywhere!'

Writing at the same time, C. E. Callwell said:

'The new-fangled ideas that had gained approval in the regiment with regard to rifled guns were frowned upon by some members of its ranks. Older members looking on them with suspicion.'

One very distinguished veteran who had performed good and gallant service in the Kaffir and Crimean Wars and had played a prominent role in the Mutiny used to grumble: 'First of all they insisted on having a lot of grooves in the bore of the gun, now they are only going to have three grooves in the bore of the gun. Please goodness that they will next have no grooves at all and we shall get back to the good old smooth-bore which was all that was necessary to beat the Russians and smash the Mutiny.'

In 1866 the Committee carried out further tests and, in recommending the adoption of muzzle-loading field guns, reported:

'...that the balance of advantages is in favour of muzzle-loading field guns.'

At a time when the rest of Europe realized that breech-loading guns were a great step forward, the British Services were reverting to muzzle-loaders although it must be said in the fairly conducted trials the muzzle-loaders had held their own in range, accuracy and rapidity of fire and, most important to the Government, they were simpler and therefore less costly than the breech-loaders.

Yet another Committee carried out tests in 1870 and again came out strongly in favour of the muzzle-loader, their report was backed by the Director of Artillery: 'The majority of Royal Artillery officers were convinced that no system of breech-loading was necessary in the field.' All the claims made for muzzle-loaders seemed to be justified when it was reported that more than 200 Krupp guns (all breech-loaders) of the Prussian Army had failed through defective breech mechanisms during their war against France.

Probably because of the cost involved, the conversion took some time and many Armstrong breech-loaders remained in service for a long period, particularly in the Colonies. By 1869 a 9 pdr rifled muzzle-loader was approved as the field gun for India; it was made of bronze because it was intended that India should make their own guns and bronze guns were simpler to manufacture than wrought-iron, built-up guns. Also, there was a need for mobility and a bronze 6 pdr weighed about 6 cwt compared with 17 cwt for a cast-iron 6 pdr. Although smooth-bore guns had disappeared from service by 1870, they were still in use in India for a considerable period after this. Guns of bronze (gunmetal) were preferred for foreign or mountainous service for many years and some 3 pdr smooth-bores, machined out to 3 inches in the bore and rifled on the French system, were issued as the 7 pdr Mk I for the Bhutan Expedition in 1865. Considered too heavy, a 7 pdr Mk II was produced and adopted by both the Army and Navy, being the last brass-bound gun in the service. A final design was submitted at Woolwich as late as 1871 but it was not proceeded with and all brass ordnance was withdrawn from service in 1874.

In 1871 an iron 9 pdr 8 cwt Mark I rifled muzzle-loader was adopted for Horse Artillery and a 16 pdr rifled muzzle-loader for field artillery, both with wrought-iron carriages. Burrows had a few of these guns with him at Maiwand in 1880 and found them superior in range and accuracy to the more numerous Afghan smooth-bores (directed by Russian artillery officers) although much of their advantage vanished when ranges decreased to 1,000 yards and lower. Iron was preferred to wood as the material for the axle tree and trail of the travelling gun-carriage. The Armstrong rifled breech-loading guns were the last to have wooden carriages although in a few years the wrought iron was superseded by steel, the 13 pdr rifled muzzle-loader and the two 25-in. rifled muzzle-loader being among the first to be equipped with steel carriages. From 1865 to 1880, some fifty different sizes and weights of rifled muzzle-loading guns were introduced into the Royal Artillery and Royal Navy. They were generally classified as:

Mountain or Boat guns (the 2·5-in. jointed gun and the 7 pdr)

Field or Boat guns (the 9, 13 and 16 pdr guns)

Siege or Position guns (the 25 and 40 pdr and the 6·6 inch)

Medium guns (the 64 pdr; the 64 cwt, 7-in. 90 cwt and all converted smooth-bore guns)

Heavy guns (the 7-in. of 6½ tons to the 17·72 in. of 100 tons weight).

Fig. 67. Heavy gun and team of an Elephant Battery of the Royal Artillery. (Photograph by H. Bremner.)

Many of these classifications played prominent parts in the Colonial campaigns of the period, such as in the storming of the fort of Ali Musjid during the 2nd Afghan War 1878 '... the attack on Ali Musjid began with an advance by the 81st Regiment and the 14th Sikhs throwing forward a line of skirmishers to clear the villages and cover the mountain spur; a battery of 9 pdrs got into position a mile and three-quarters from Ali Musjid. Mule-batteries came thundering and clattering along the stony bed of the Khyber River and up to the open ground while the heavy 40 pdr guns were dragged forward like toys by a train of elephants. The booming of the guns and the crash of exploding shells woke the echoes of the hills on every hand while spurts of white smoke from the line of skirmishers darted incessantly forward. Before long the guns of the fort were completely silenced and the troops began their advance to the deep hoarse booming of the 40 pdrs reverberating from hill to hill.' Roberts laboriously dragged four 40 pdrs on his epic march from Kabul to Kandahar and earlier, at Peiwar Kotal, came up against Afghans well armed with artillery

'18 pdr cannon, waggons, ammunition boxes and piles of shells and round-shot lay in all directions. However, their gunners had much to learn in the proper adjustment of time-fuses; at least fifty per cent. of their shells exploded in the air.'

The Franco-Prussian War emphasized the need for mobility in artillery and the value of well-trained Horse Artillery to be employed with cavalry and so required to be more mobile than Field Artillery. In consequence the lighter gun (the 9 pdr 6 cwt) was introduced in 1874; the gunners, who in field artillery normally rode on the gun and limber seats, were horsed as outriders; and the 6-horse team was employed instead of a 4-horse team.

Throughout this period, rearmament of British coast defences had made very slow progress, mainly due to lack of funds. By 1870 many of the more important batteries in British coast fortresses had been armed with improvised pieces such as smooth-bore 32 pdrs while 8-in. guns became RML 64 pdrs and SB 68 pdrs (10-inch) became RML 80 pdrs, following upon a suggestion made in 1863 by Captain Palliser that the old cast-iron, smooth-bore guns should be re-lined with wrought-iron rifled tubes. Thus hundreds of obsolete guns were given a new lease of life and could perform useful service, even so these pieces, mounted upon every description of carriage and slide (common standing, casemate, dwarf, etc.), could not compare with the up-to-date equipment of the land artillery. It was not until the Naval manoeuvres of 1887-88-89 had shown that commercial ports along the English coast were vulnerable that three million pounds was voted for coastal defence and 6-in. and 10-in. breech-loading guns were provided.

The 9 pdr and 16 pdr RML guns, considered to be inferior to foreign artillery, were replaced in 1878 by a 13 pdr RML gun for both Horse and Field and a 2·5 in. RML for Mountain Artillery. Possessing the greater length of barrel made possible by slow burning powder, both these guns represented a great advance in design and the 2·5 had a two-part barrel which screwed together and made its name as the famous 'screw-gun'. Due to excessive recoil the 13 pdr was unpopular. This gun was fitted with axle-tree seats with the idea of giving increased facilities to the field gunner by making it possible for two members of the gun detachment, in addition to the 'Number One', to remain with the gun and in an emergency, work it alone while waiting for the remainder of the detachment. In 1882 the Corps of Royal Artillery drivers vanished as enlistment of 'gunner and driver' ensured that every man was trained to perform both duties.

By the 1880s the artillery scene was rapidly changing as experts began to realize that muzzle-loading was obsolete – a decision forced upon them by improvements in breech construction and difficulties of loading the longer barrelled muzzle-loading guns. Perhaps it had been noticed that in the early 1870s a 7-in. muzzle-loader weighing 7 tons had fired a 115 lb. shell 4,800 yards whereas a 7-in. breech-loader weighing only 4 tons 2 cwt fired a 90 lb. shell 4,000 yards. In this period the largest muzzle-loader made at Woolwich was a 68 ton gun of 13·5 in. calibre. Lord Armstrong, the indomitable champion of the breech-loader, left no stone unturned to persuade the Government to change from muzzle to breech-loading and invited the Admiralty and the War Office to test two of his new breech-loaders, a 6-inch and an 8-inch. Both were designed to make the best use of the discoveries of Nobel and Abel regarding the burning-speed of charges and the length of muzzle. It was not the lessons of war but these impressive trials together with innovations in the armaments of foreign services that persuaded the Government, in 1881, to once again adopt breech-loading guns for the Royal Horse Artillery and Field Brigades.

They were issued with guns constructed as far as was practical on the muzzle-loading 13 pdr which, in spite of its faults, was considered to be one of the finest specimens of British ordnance. Weighing only 8½ cwt, the calibre at the bore was 3 inches enlarged to 6½ inches in the powder chamber, the fittings were of bronze (formerly called gun-metal) but the gun itself, including the whole of the barrel, was chiefly of steel and only in the rear were wrought-iron coils shrunk on to strengthen and support it. In 1867 the Armstrong method of building-up guns with many thin coils had been superseded by a method of using a few heavy coils giving the same strength but much easier to manufacture. By 1884 the popularity of steel caused it to replace wrought-iron in the manufacture of guns and the heavy coils were replaced by steel hoops which in their turn gave place to steel wire in a method that gave a greater tensile strength.

By 1885 both Horse and Field Artillery had been equipped with a 12 pdr breech-loading gun of 3-in. calibre weighing 7 cwt. Drawn by six horses, the gun, carriage and limber when fully packed weighed about 38 cwt and proved to be too heavy for the R.H.A. so a new 12 pdr BL gun of 6 cwt with a simple, light carriage was introduced in 1894.

Checking the movement of the carriage along the ground after firing put a heavy strain on the gunners who had to run the gun up to its original position after each time of firing and in many battles, such as Waterloo, firing suffered towards the end of the action because of the fatigued gunners. The rate of

Fig. 68. A group of gunners around a Whitworth gun, c. 1864.

fire of a gun was diminished by the difficulty of checking this recoil, a problem which taxed many minds during the last quarter of the nineteenth century. A higher rate of fire was made possible by a much simpler and more easily operated breech mechanism together with control of recoil through the charge being contained in a brass cartridge case, instead of silk-cloth bags as formerly, which expanded and acted as a seal for the gas at the breech when the gun was fired. These innovations were introduced in a 12 pdr quick-firing gun mounted on a pedestal set in a concrete bed, followed by 4·7 in. and 6-in. quick-firing guns (all breech-loading guns) mounted in the same way, which were installed in 1892 as coastal defence to deal with raids by torpedo craft.

As early as 1869 a hydraulic buffer had been tried out by the Navy and coast defence in which the resistance of water flowing through a small hole was employed to check recoil; later, strong spiral springs were used for the same purpose. Applying the same principle to mobile artillery added so much weight as to impair mobility and emphasized the problem of devising a suitable travelling carriage which could control recoil – one of the main difficulties of equipping Horse and Field Artillery with the Quick Firer. The early 12 pdr breech-loader 7 cwt gun used a shoe-brake which partially solved the problem but, although the gun was prevented from running back, it imparted such a rigidity to the whole of the piece and carriage that the violent kick when the gun was fired

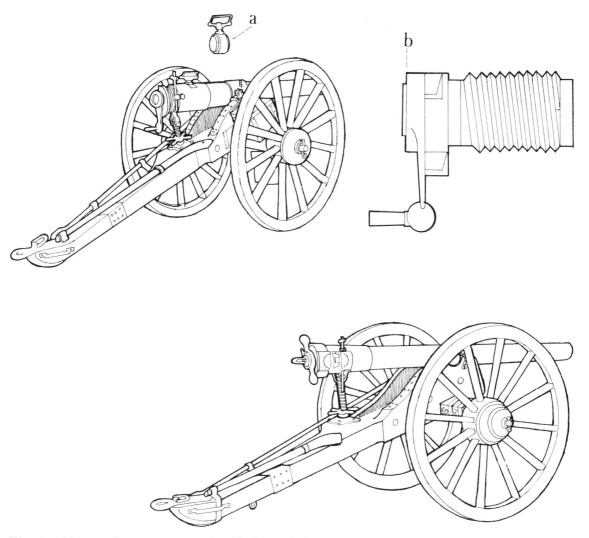

Fig. 69. Above: *Armstrong 12-pdr-rifled breech-loading gun 1859:* (a) *Vent piece;* (b) *Breech.* Below: *Whitworth 12-pdr-rifled breech-loading gun.*

made it necessary to re-lay it for each round. The shoe-brake remained the only means of checking recoil in the lighter field pieces until 1899 when it was replaced by the axle-spade, a slight improvement made necessary by the demands of the war in South Africa.

When France re-armed in 1896–97 it was rumoured that they had a real quick-firer of 75 mm. calibre capable of firing twenty to thirty rounds per minute. The French managed to retain the secrets of the famous 'soixante-quinze' so that it was some years before this could be confirmed. The French re-arming and the increasing threat of Germany aroused sufficient alarm in Britain to cause the appointment of Sir Henry

Brackenbury, the Director-General of Ordnance, to advise on the re-arming of the artillery. His startling recommendation that obsolete equipment should be replaced over three years instead of the usual ten years transitional period was adopted without reservation. Unfortunately British manufacturers could not take up the challenge with sufficient rapidity so Sir Henry, as an *ad interim* measure, placed an order with a German firm for enough guns, limbers, stores, spare parts and 500 rounds per gun to equip eighteen batteries. This Düsseldorf maker had recently demonstrated a 15 pdr in which the recoil was so adequately taken up by the top carriage that a coin placed on the gun wheel had not been shaken off when the gun was fired.

With the Boer War still dragging on, British gun-makers were invited to submit designs and, by 1902, a number of specimen quick-firers were on trial. Unfortunately they all had some feature that made them unsuitable for service. Undaunted, the Committee took the unprecedented step of inviting the various firms to co-operate in producing a composite quick-firer gun from the best features of all those submitted. By 1903 four complete batteries of 13 pdr and 18 pdr guns were ready for trial; they embodied an Armstrong wire-wound gun, with a Vickers recoil arrangement and Ordnance factories sighting and elevating gear and ammunition-carrying system. Completely successful, the 18 pdr was one of the most used guns during World War I, firing nearly 100 million rounds as compared with $1\frac{1}{2}$ million rounds by the 13 pdr. By the summer of 1906 seven divisions at home had been equipped and the field artillery took on a new lease of life with the knowledge that their new first-class weapons would be used to the best advantage with all the tactical knowledge gained during the Boer War.

Used both as a propellant and as a bursting charge for shells throughout the whole era of smooth-bore artillery, gunpowder merely exploded and did not detonate like modern high explosives. Gunpowder was a mixture of saltpetre, sulphur and charcoal which exploded when ignited producing large quantities of gas in the process and apart from national variations in the different qualities of charcoal, its composition remained stable throughout the eighteenth and nineteenth centuries. Because of its vulnerability to dampness soldiers were traditionally adjured to 'keep their powder dry'. A fixed weight propellant charge for each type of gun was made into a cartridge for easier transportation and handling. During the eighteenth century the cartridges were enclosed in paper, then flannel was used later replaced by serge – both fabrics were totally consumed on firing so obviating the danger of burning fragments remaining in the bore. Mortars, whose range was altered by adjusting the weight of the charge,

were always loaded with loose powder.

During the gunpowder era, the danger of explosion was always present and there are many recorded instances of magazines exploding in fortresses and ammunition waggons blowing up on the march because of loose powder being ignited by friction. Because of its inflammable nature, all implements used by gunners were made of wood and copper and, to minimize the risk of accidents, drills for loading and firing were rigorously practised. Men of British gun detachments were numbered consecutively, the NCO in command usually being known as 'Number One'. The ventsman and the firer stood behind the wheels on either side of the piece while the spongeman and the loader stood similarly in front of the wheels. Up to four other men, depending on the type of gun, prepared and supplied the loader with ammunition.

After a round had been fired, the spongeman wetted the end of the long spongestaff in his water bucket and thrust it down the bore to extinguish any smouldering fragments of powder or the cartridge case which might still remain there. Then, the loader placed the new charge in the muzzle and it was rammed home by the spongeman with the reverse end of his spongestaff. At the same time the ventsman 'served his vent' by placing his thumb over the hole so preventing a rush of air which might cause a premature explosion of the charge if, in spite of the sponging, any burning fragments remained in the bore. Traditionally, the spongeman was entitled to hit the ventsman on the head with the spongestaff if he failed to serve his vent. The charge rammed home, the ventsman thrust his 'pricker' (a sharp-pointed instrument) down the vent and pierced the fabric enclosing the charge, to make ignition more certain. Meanwhile, the projectile had been placed in the muzzle by the loader and rammed home against the charge by the spongeman. With the piece laid on its target, all was now ready for firing.

For more than 250 years the most reliable method of firing guns was by using the linstock and the portfire. The linstock was a continuously burning slow-match (it burnt

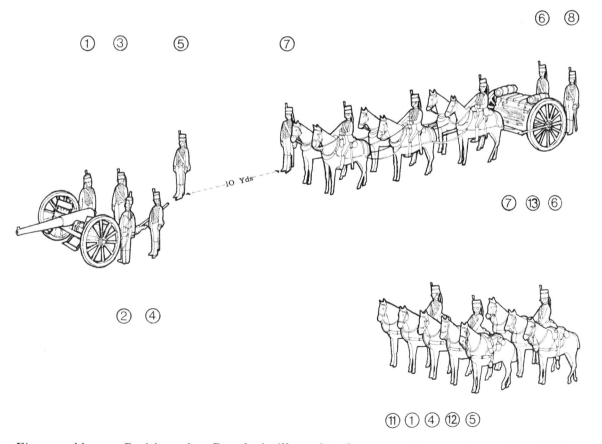

Fig. 70. Above: *Position of a Royal Artillery detachment on the march, c. 1890*. Below: *Positions of a Royal Horse Artillery detachment armed with breech-loading ordnance, c. 1890. The detachment horses and holders (Nos. 11–13) were usually posted behind the limber (see also Fig. 64)*.

Fig. 71. Colonel Acklam's troop of the Royal Horse Artillery photographed on parade at Rawalpindi in December 1864.

Fig. 72. Guns and limbers of a troop of horse artillery being cleaned after a field day, c. 1890.

Fig. 73. A Royal Horse Artillery troop on parade at Shorncliffe Camp, 1885.

at the rate of one yard in eight or nine hours) made of three loosely woven strands of hemp boiled in lees of old wine or a solution of wood ash or saltpetre, the whole bound together with an outer layer of hemp strands. This was loosely wound around the linstock itself and was lit when the order 'prepare for action' was given. Provided on a scale of one for two guns and often carried by the officers, the linstock was often of ornamental design, having a spiked end so that it could be planted in the ground.

The means whereby the flame was transferred from the linstock to the vent, the portfire, was a stiff tube some 16½ inches long made of layers of paper containing a composition which burnt at the rate of one inch per minute. Immediately before firing, the firer ignited his portfire from the linstock and stood by the gun while it was being loaded. When the order to fire was given, he applied the portfire to the vent which had been primed earlier by the ventsman by pouring a little loose powder into the hole.

In due course, this practice became a likely source of premature explosions as it caused the vent to become eroded and enlarged. The portfire was extinguished by the firer cutting off the burning end with the portfire cutter, which was permanently mounted on the trail of the carriage.

This system of firing was still in use during the Napoleonic Wars although in 1807 a percussion powder was invented ignited by a blow; subsequently a firing gear was designed to make use of this discovery and was used in British service by 1840. A friction tube introduced in 1853 had a roughened strip of metal pulled through composition in the outer end of the tube which caused it to ignite and pass a flash down the tube to the charge. Both percussion and friction tubes were in service during the Crimean War but the old portfire was still held in reserve and was used throughout the Indian Mutiny.

The dependence of muzzle-loading guns on gunpowder was accompanied by such risks on the gun position that the most rigorous devotion to gun drill was always necessary. In action the risks were increased by the danger of a shell or bullet striking the ammunition waggon causing it to explode. During the Battle of Ferozeshah in 1846 the explosion of these waggons caused great loss of ammunition during the first day of the battle. Both gun crews and horses suffered casualties by explosions both in and out of action, the ventsman was always vulnerable because he carried pouches containing a large number of readily inflammable tubes on his person.

Smooth-bore, muzzle-loading guns fired three types of ammunition – roundshot, case or canister and common shell. Loading was speeded up and the danger obviated of burning fragments remaining in the bore by attaching the cartridge to the projectile so that both could be loaded together. Although a routine procedure in the Artillery of the United States by 1840, British Artillery kept the charge and projectile separate, except those of caseshot, although time was saved by ramming both charge and projectile together.

The most useful projectile throughout the whole era of smooth-bore artillery, roundshot could destroy walls, gates, guns and waggons and, able to slice men and horses in half were devastating against them particularly when they were in the open, en masse or taken in enfilade. Roundshot could be seen in flight by the target men who were often unable to evade them because of their close order formation – at the Alma a group of fifteen men were killed by the same roundshot while standing precisely in its line of fire. In order to produce its greatest effect, roundshot had to arrive at its target with a high remaining velocity and a flat trajectory so that normally it was fired only from guns and not howitzers. Between 70/80 per cent. of the ammunition carried by British Artillery was roundshot fixed to a 'sabot' – a circular plate of hardwood (usually elm) – which fitted the bore and was fastened to the projectile with tin straps although, by the 1850s, it was usually rivetted in place. Although considerably burnt as it passed up the bore, this sabot prevented the shot from rolling or turning over and helped to seal the gas behind it. Providing its calibre was suitable, roundshot could be picked up and fired back at its original owners. During the Indian Mutiny when the British force at the siege of Delhi ran short of 18 pdr roundshot, they had foragers go out to pick up, with great care, the still-hot roundshot that had arrived from the defenders. On Delhi Ridge two 24 pdr guns captured from the mutineers were so short of shot that they had to rely on firing the spent missiles of the 24 pdrs fired at them by the mutineers – natives were paid half a rupee for every roundshot they brought in.

Almost anything could be fired out of smooth-bore, muzzle-loading guns – besieged in a fortified house at Arrah during the Indian Mutiny a small party of Englishmen fired doorhandles at the enemy when their roundshot ran out!

Because of its narrow line of fire, solid shot was not always particularly effective against infantry or cavalry making a frontal assault. In such a situation the guns were loaded with canister or caseshot, which consisted of a tin containing of the same size as the bore, filled with cast bullets. The case burst open as it left the muzzle of the gun allowing the bullets to spread out in an arc over the frontage of the gun from which it was fired. The size and number of bullets used in caseshot varied considerably and by 1850 the caseshot of the field pieces contained:

9 pdr gun	41 5-oz. bullets.
6 pdr gun	41 $1\frac{1}{4}$-oz. bullets.
24 pdr howitzer	100 2-oz. bullets.

The efficiency of caseshot was determined in trials by firing at a screen as high as a man's head and about 120 feet wide, representing the frontage over which a single battery would develop its fire when in action. At 250 yards range 75 per cent. of the 9 pdr and 30 per cent. of the 6 pdr bullets hit the target and at 150 yards the 9 pdr scored 65 per cent. hits and the 6 pdr 55 per cent. As enemy troops closed in on the final stages of an attack, it was possible to fire two charges of caseshot simultaneously from a single

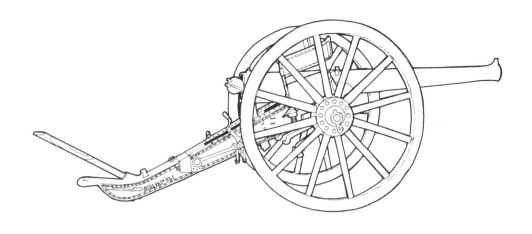

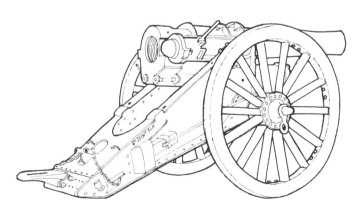

Fig. 74. Above: *12-pdr R.B.L. field gun, c. 1890.* Centre: *9-pdr R.M.L. field gun, c. 1882.*
Below: *6-in. B.L. Howitzer, c. 1900.*

93

gun. It was most effective at close ranges up to about 300 yards so that it must be classified as a defensive weapon.

Common shell, the design of which hardly changed from 1750 to 1860, was fired from the smaller howitzers and mortars. It was never particularly effective, due to the lack of an efficient fuse to impose the correct delay period between the moment of firing the gun and the arrival of the shell at the target when the explosive filling of the shell was ignited and the projectile forced to burst. Fired by the 10 in. and 13-in. mortars the larger shells burst most spectacularly, particularly in the 1850s when accurate and reliable fuses had been developed.

In 1784, Lieutenant Henry Shrapnel RA, produced the first spherical caseshot, consisting of a hollow iron ball containing a number of bullets together with a bursting charge and fuse to cause it to explode at the correct point on its trajectory. This shell was devised to fill the need for a projectile that had all the effects of caseshot but with an increased range through the shot bursting far up its trajectory instead of at the muzzle. Used quite effectively during the Napoleonic Wars with an improved design of fuse developed by Captain Boxer RA, the shrapnel shell was retained in the British service after the Waterloo period. In 1837, trials were held at Woolwich to determine the effective range of the shrapnel shell and in the 1850s it was generally accepted that the projectile was effective at between 300 and 1,100 yards range. The trials revealed that field gun shells, each containing sixty bullets, could be expected to obtain seventeen hits on figure targets at 1,100 yards range. The shell of siege guns containing 150 bullets would obtain sixty hits at the same range.

Until 1849 in Europe and 1858 in India, the fuse fitted into the hole in the shell casing consisted of a wooden tube with a ribbed outer surface, the ribs being so spaced as to give a burning time of half a second, the fuse being cut at the appropriate rib before being placed in the shell. Each British light-gun detachment had four gunners concerned solely with cutting the fuse and rasping to make it fit into the shell, cutting the fuse

before coming into action to such lengths as they anticipated would be needed and stacking the rounds in batches ready for use. By the 1840s, pre-set fuses were being issued for selection on the gun position. Surprisingly good results were obtained with this seemingly primitive fuse when it was used with common shell that had been 'set short' for air bursts. If the shell was required to burst on the ground, fuse length was not so important because it did not matter greatly if the projectile remained lying on the ground with its fuse spluttering before bursting.

With the introduction of spherical case an effective time-fuse became necessary because the strength of the projectile lay in its ability to burst at the right point on its trajectory. In 1849, Captain Boxer invented an improved fuse, consisting of a wooden cone with a centre channel of powder and side channels (filled with pistol powder) with radial holes bored into them at close intervals, representing fractions of time. These holes were stopped with clay and the whole fuse covered with paper, numbered at the appropriate holes. To set the fuse to the required length of burning, a hole was bored straight through to the centre channel and the fuse then placed in the shell. When fired, the flash from the propellant charge passed over the whole of the shell and ignited the powder in the centre channel, which burned down until the bored hole was reached, sending a flash down the side channel, into the shell and exploding it.

Carcasses had been in use for some years and, by the time of the Crimean War, it was possible to fire one that burned on the ground and another which contained a parachute allowing the light ball (which could burn for as long as 15 minutes) to descend slowly after it had been ignited at the top of its trajectory.

The relative effectiveness of these projectiles is shown by the scales of ammunition held for British Light Artillery, which remained almost unchanged from 1800 to 1860, being based on the practical experience of the Napoleonic Wars. As given in *British Smooth-Bore Artillery* by Major-General B. P. Hughes (1969), these scales are shown in the first part of the table.

SCALES OF AMMUNITION HELD FOR BRITISH LIGHT ARTILLERY

Rounds per gun in the firing battery

	Round	*Case*	*Spherical*	*Common*	*Carcass*
6 pr. gun	149	19	26	—	—
9 pr. gun	86/92*	16	24/20*	—	—
12 pr. howitzer	—	8	68	56	4
24 pr. howitzer	—	8	42	32	2

* Changed about 1830.

Proportions including the first-line ammunition (i.e. that carried in additional ammunition waggons) are given in the second part of the table.

Additional first-line scale

6 pr. gun	77%	$9\frac{1}{2}$%	$13\frac{1}{2}$%	—	—
9 pr. gun	70%	$11\frac{1}{2}$%	$18\frac{1}{2}$%	—	—
12 pr. howitzer	—	5%	50%	42%	3%
24 pr. howitzer	—	8%	50%	39%	3%

In India the natures both of the country and of the fighting in it led to the artilleries of the East India Company holding a lower proportion of round shot and a larger quantity of the other types, as shown in the third part of the table.

Indian scale

	Gun	*Round*	*Case*	*Spherical*
Bengal Artillery (1830)	9 pr.	$66\frac{1}{2}$%	$7\frac{1}{2}$%	26%
Madras Artillery	9 pr.	53%	$17\frac{1}{2}$%	$19\frac{1}{2}$%

Considerable progress was made in this field during the 1860s when spherical shot and shell were replaced by elongated projectiles fired by the new rifled guns. Armstrong introduced segment shell, common shell and case shell. A cross between case and shrapnel, segment shell was constructed of a thin cast-iron case covering rows of cast-iron segments enclosing a bursting shell. Common shells were explosive, nose-fused or base-fused and filled with gunpowder. During this period, Colonel Boxer greatly improved the shrapnel shell. The improved armour on warships resulted in the invention of an armour-piercing shell.

Between 1870 and 1883 fuse design improved considerably as a wooden time fuse with a reliable detonator was introduced and later replaced with a metal 'time and concussion fuse'.

To combat the excessive erosion in the bore of the gun due to the use of studded projectiles a copper 'gas jet' was adopted in 1878 and a little later the copper driving band was introduced as a component part of the shell, being essentially the same as the driving band of today.

In 1878 star shells of a new pattern were introduced into the Service, to be fired from a 6.3 in. mortar. Each shell contained twenty-one magnesium stars which, when exploded in the air lighted up – for a few minutes – a large tract of country with great brilliance. They proved most successful during the wars in Afghanistan and on the North-West Frontier.

In 1880 for the most part shells were made of cast-iron, but in this year shrapnel for the 2.5 gun was constructed of cast steel and from then on steel began to replace iron for both guns and projectiles.

Both in the Afghan Wars of 1879–80 and in the Sudan Campaign, shrapnel played a big part in defeating the native opponents. In April 1880, at Ahmed Kheyl, Stewart's force of 7,000 were so rapidly attacked by Afghans that the artillery, after opening fire at 1,200 yards had to reduce range to 400 yards and then, with tribesmen on top of them, the guns were loaded with shrapnel, heads towards the charge so that they exploded at the muzzle. The ground before the guns was covered with heaps of torn and mutilated dead and dying. At Tamai in 1884, when the Dervishes broke into the British square, the gunners of the battery of four guns were left without protection and were heavily assailed by crowds of tribesmen but officers and men stood firm to their guns and mowed down the on-rushing Dervishes with shrapnel.

In 1882, shortly after cordite had been adopted, a Committee was assembled who considered the fact that the new smokeless propellant was much more powerful than gunpowder and so provided an opportunity of adding to the weight of the shell without any radical alteration to the actual gun. Subsequently they recommended that the 12 pdr of 7 cwt should be converted into a 15 pdr and eventually field artillery was issued with a converted gun with shrapnel as its only shell. The 12 pdr of 6 cwt and the 15 pdr constituted the armaments of the Horse and Field Artillery (apart from field howitzer batteries) when the forces were mobilized for the South African War in 1899.

The abolition of common shell for field guns gave rise to a demand for some form of artillery allowing greater shell power in the field, because it had been voiced that the field gun ought to fire a projectile heavier than 12 lbs – the common shell of that weight having little effect on earthworks. In 1896 field howitzer batteries were formed, armed with a 5-in. B.L. howitzer firing a 50 lb. shell. For siege artillery, a 6-in. B.L. howitzer took the place of the muzzle-loading guns and howitzers, to become practically the sole weapon of the siege train.

In 1898 a new high explosive 'lyddite' was introduced to replace gunpowder as a shell filling. It was adopted for the bursting charge of common shell for all natures of breech-loading guns and howitzers of over 4.7 in. calibre. It was fired for the first time in war at Omdurman in 1898. Here the artillery included some 5-in. howitzers, little stubby guns painted pea-soup colour, that bombarded Omdurman with 50 lb. shells at a range of 3,000 yards, tearing great holes in the dome of the Mahdi's tomb, bringing down the cupolas and enveloping the whole structure in a cloud of yellow fumes and dust. The effect of lyddite was awe-inspiring.

The end of the seventeenth century saw the adoption of a method for moving wheeled ordnance that lasted well into the present century. The trail was hooked to a two-wheeled vehicle – a limber, to which draft animals could be harnessed. The joint between the rear end of the trail and limber allowed great play so that the limber and gun carriage were very mobile even over the roughest ground while the limber itself could carry large boxes of equipment. At various times artillery has been drawn by virtually every animal capable of pulling a vehicle, particularly those to hand in the specific theatre of war, although the horse was by far the most widely used draught animal for artillery. During the nineteenth century all British carriages were drawn by even-numbered teams of horses:

4-horse teams drew 24 cwts.

6-horse teams drew 30 cwts.

Fig. 75. Royal Artillery, c. 1890. Above: *'Action-Front'*. Below: *On the march.*

8-horse teams drew 36 cwts.

12-horse teams drew 38 cwts.

By 1850 British horse teams had become standardized so that the 18 pdr gun was pulled by twelve horses; the 9 pdr, 24 pdr and 32 pdr howitzer by eight horses and the 7 pdr gun and 12 pdr howitzer by six horses.

Those animals linked by traces nearest to the limber were the 'wheelers' and their task was to support the limber and hold it steady in the vertical plane while steering it horizontally. This was done by either having a pair of shafts projecting from the limber on either side of one of the wheelers or by a single pole attached to the limber and passing between the two wheelers. In both methods the limber followed the wheelers when they turned, the front ends of the shaft or pole being held in position by being attached to the harness of the wheelers.

Riding on the near-side horses, the drivers controlled the off-side or 'hand' horses by reins and a short whip pressed against the hand horses neck to urge him forward to the left. The hand wheeler was between off-set shafts and neck collars were used. Using lively ungelded horses in short supply, during the first half of the nineteenth century the Bengal Artillery placed gunners on the backs of all three hand horses of the gun team and of the waggon team, so that pole draught had to be used. This may well have been the same '... batt'ry of the corps' at Ferozeshah that features in Kipling's *Snarleyow*!

To attain greater mobility, the nineteenth-century practice of seating two men on the gun-limber ceased in British Horse Artillery early in the twentieth century. In British field batteries up to six men could be carried on the waggon body and its limber with two more on the gun limber but, to save the horses, it was only done in an emergency. However, at the Alma the British field battery hurried forward into a position which dominated the Russian gun areas and then had to be brought into action by the mounted officers and the staff of the Artillery Commander because its panting detachments were quite unable to keep up with the guns. The Bengal Artillery and the British Artillery of the East India Company had two seats on the axle-tree of the gun carrying two men facing to the rear with their feet supported by the hanging breast chains – a very uncomfortable position!

The bullock, intensely reliable although slow, was much used in India as an artillery draught animal because it was a tough animal unaffected by the noise of battle. Harnessed in pairs, bullocks pulled vehicles through a yoke resting on their necks and pushed by their humps, the yokes were connected to chain traces running to the front of the limber which was supported by a pole with its front end fastened to the yokes of the wheel bullocks by a loose coupling. The wheel bullocks were driven by a man seated on the limber while the other drivers walked alongside each pair of the team. In 1859 as many as twenty pairs of bullocks were used to draw a 24 pdr siege gun but twelve pairs were normally considered enough for these heavy pieces. Bullock teams took over guns from elephants once the area of battle was reached because the larger animals were unreliable under fire and often ran away. Otherwise, the highly intelligent and capable elephants were much employed in India to draw artillery. Used in tandem to pull heavy siege guns on the march, two elephants drew each carriage, and if the gun got stuck the lead elephant was unhooked and pushed with his forehead against the gun muzzle. During the Lushai Expedition of 1871, the forty-six elephants of the artillery and commissariat stampeded after being fired on by natives. It was not until the following day that they were finally rounded up with three missing. Sometimes mules were used to draw artillery carriages and a camel battery unsuccessfully took part in the First Afghan War of 1839.

On various occasions, most of the animals detailed above drew the variety of carts and waggons that accompanied batteries of artillery. The most important waggon was that carrying the ammunition but spare wheels were most valuable because a wooden gun wheel was perhaps the most vulnerable part of the gun and a badly damaged wheel could put a weapon out of action and render it immovable.

The gun-layers were usually the most experienced men of the detachment who, using very crude sights to lay their smooth-bore guns and howitzers by eye, showed considerable skill and accuracy. The piece was laid by looking along the barrel and lining it on the target and, by manhandling the trail of the gun, traversing until a correct line was attained. Great reliance was placed on the layer's visual estimate, particularly with the lighter guns where both range and elevation were small, although the performance of each gun was carefully recorded during practice firing and range tables were produced.

The advances in artillery that followed the Franco-Prussian War made it obvious that field artillery needed a reliable range-finder; the great technical advance made in gunnery had completely outdated the old system of guessing ranges. The reliable range-finder adopted in 1890 was soon out-moded by the complete change in tactics brought about by the Boer War that prevented the gunner from having a clear view, over open sights, of the target. It became necessary to introduce a system of sighting where the fire of the guns was controlled by a layer who could not see the target. The first of these improvised sights was the 'Gunners Arc' which, although very primitive in construction, embodied the elements of the sighting system used today.

Because the layer could no longer see his target some means had to be found to get all guns in a battery pointing in the same direction. Known as 'laying out the line' the method was to plant the aiming-posts of the directing gun in the line indicated by the post planted by the battery commander. Trailing lengths of cord corresponding to the distances from the aiming-posts on their flank, gunners from the other guns went forward to plant their own aiming-posts in front, then their second posts in the rear. The guns, now parallel, were brought into action in the line of their own aiming-posts. When targets were engaged, an observation officer (posted on a crest) observed the fall of shot and ordered the necessary realignment of the guns. Between 1902 and 1910, various appliances were tried before a workable system was evolved and the old 'fishing tackle' drill became obsolete.

In his book *History of the Royal Artillery 1860–1914*, Major-General Sir John Headlam RA, wrote: 'In studying the records of those eventful years and analyzing the many changes they brought, the most puzzling enigma is the strange slowness of the generation that first received rifled guns to grasp the potentialities of their new weapons. How was it that the Royal Artillery – alone of European artilleries – made no effort to suit its gunnery or its tactics to its new armament?'

The tactical employment of artillery had completely failed to keep pace with the remarkable technical advances in artillery of the last half of the nineteenth century. In 1899 the Royal Artillery took the field in South Africa trained to mass their guns in the open and to first silence the enemy artillery before supporting the infantry attack by turning the guns on to the enemy firing line. Against the Boers this resulted in heavy losses from invisible guns and rifles fired by natural marksmen with innate talent for concealment. Their well-aimed rifle fire caused heavy casualties among the gunners so that the guns were fitted with shields to protect them. This heresy, this untraditional course aroused a great outcry in the Press, similar to that which occurred in 1891 when it was suggested that guns should be painted khaki!

The British practice of siting their guns out in the open could have resulted in their crews being almost wiped out had the Boers been sufficiently experienced in the use of artillery to concentrate their guns and to methodically range them. Learning from experience and, for the first time, taking advantage of the new smokeless powder, guns soon began to be sited in concealed positions. It is frightening to consider what could have happened to British artillerymen during the early part of World War I but for the valuable experience gained during the Boer War.

The last word on the guns of the Victorian period concerns not British weapons but those of foreign enemies. The *Army and Navy Gazette* of August 1879 contains the following paragraph:

'It is a matter of regret that no steps are taken to preserve the numerous handsome ornamental guns lying on the wharfs of the Royal Arsenal at Woolwich. Most of these have been captured from the enemy, in Europe, Asia, Africa and America; many are interesting from the inscriptions on them. It is strange that neither the Royal Regiment of Artillery nor the War Office seem to appreciate such relics. In any other country but England, they would have been preserved and carefully looked after, and would adorn the entrances to any Military Academy, or to such a mess establishment and barracks as Woolwich boasts of.'

Fig. 76. Royal Artillery, Mountain Battery, c. 1846. No. 5 in the set of coloured lithographs after G. B. Campion.

Fig. 77. Indian troops assembling a 2·5 Mountain gun. (Photograph by H. Bremner.)

MOUNTAIN GUNS

The majority of wars fought by Britain during Queen Victoria's reign were relatively small Colonial campaigns where the terrain, conditions and circumstances precluded the use of anything other than light artillery, usually the mountain guns. The hillmen of India's North-West Frontier said that what they feared was '... not the child-rifle but the devil guns which killed half a dozen men with one shot which burst and threw out splinters as deadly as the shot themselves.'

Just how much respect the hillmen had for the mountain guns was indicated during operations against the Mohmands in 1879. It is reported that on arriving at Kam Dakka, Captain Creagh and his 130 Native troops found that the villagers were very reluctant to allow the troops to enter their village and said they had neither asked for and did not require any assistance; they further expressed the view that the detachment would be defeated as it did not possess any mountain guns. In the same operations, the column advancing to relieve Captain Creagh brought their mountain guns into action and shelled an enclosure with common-shell and percussion fuses, a shell from each gun burst in the middle of the enclosure and the standards disappeared; as the enemy fled, shrapnel was fired at them as they ran. Later the column encountered no opposition but saw a raft crossing the Kabul River and men assembling as if to embark upon it. A mountain gun fired a shell at it at a range of 1,800 yards which struck about 100 yards short

and appeared to ricochet into the raft. The enemy dispersed and shortly afterwards the raft disappeared.

An Indian mountain train, with six 3 pdr guns carried on mules, was formed for service in Afghanistan and moved up to Kabul just before the rising in 1841. Half of the battery was wiped out in the retreat from Kabul and the other half, with Brigadier Shelton's column, was besieged in Jellalabad, where it more than proved its worth. After the second Sikh War the frontiers of British India pushed forward to the foothills of the North-West Frontier and forces were required to control the tribesmen of the area. The Bengal Artillery on the frontier used elephants, camels and mules to transport their light guns, howitzers and mortars. Elephants carried the mountain guns during the Lushai expedition of 1871, but the paths were too rough for them so that native coolies had to be employed, sixteen to a gun. There were six for the 150 lb gun itself; six for the carriage; two for each wheel and four for each ammunition box (containing nine rounds).

In 1850 the first entirely mule-borne mountain train battery was organized and its success caused other batteries to be formed until a force of Mountain Artillery were stationed permanently on the frontier to serve colourfully and creditably for a hundred years. Each mule carried on its back a pack-saddle consisting of two padded panels on which was secured a saddle tree shaped to fit the various top loads. The gun and its carriage, divided into sections for transport, were either suspended from hooks on each side of the saddle tree as 'side loads' or carried as 'top loads' strapped on top of it. Using a combination of specially shaped instruments called 'lifters' and 'bearers', the gunners lifted the top loads on and off the saddles. In both British and Indian mountain batteries the gunner had to be at least 6 feet tall and of the finest physique because, as the arms had to be raised to the fully vertical position in order to clear the mule's body, strong men had to be recruited to lift the 250 lb loads on to the mule's back.

In the smooth-bore period, these batteries had a mixture of 3 pdr guns and the $4\frac{2}{5}$ in. howitzer. At first the batteries had six guns but a standard establishment of three guns and three howitzers was introduced in 1860, each being carried on three mules. The little British $4\frac{2}{5}$ in. howitzer had passed out of field service by about 1800 but remained to serve creditably in the Mountain Artillery until 1865.

These small howitzers played a prominent role during an expedition by General Neville Chamberlain against the Mahsud and Waziri tribes in the formidable Barari Tangi Pass in May 1860, defended by tribesmen behind strong stone breastworks. Three native infantry battalions advanced to the attack, supported by a 3 pdr gun and two howitzers of the mountain battery, coming into action 250 yards from the breastworks. However, the stone defences were at a much higher level than the gun position so that the roundshot glanced upward off the stone face to curve back and land *behind* the gun position! These roundshot were recovered and returned to the ammunition dump. The howitzers lobbed a number of common-shell over the breastworks, until masked by the infantry. Suddenly the tribesmen erupted over the breastworks, to pour down the hill and push the infantry back in a confused hand-to-hand combat. On the flank, the battery was unable to fire into the struggling mass of friend and foe, so the battery commander ordered charges only to be loaded, with the loaders holding the caseshot *outside* the muzzles to prevent a gun being fired too

soon in the excitement. Under a hail of bullets and stones, with the officers firing their pistols at heads appearing over the breastworks, they waited until none but tribesmen were in line of fire. At once the order to load was given, the shot rammed home and three close-range salvoes of caseshot caused great destruction in the enemy ranks, causing the shaken tribesmen to be pushed back allowing the infantry to sweep up the hill and clear the Pass.

The mountain batteries served with distinction in theatres other than the North-West Frontier. In 1868 two batteries of the A/21st Bde RA went to Abyssinia equipped with a steel 7 pdr RML gun weighing 150 lbs with a barrel length of 2 ft 2·5 inches, permitting the gun being carried across a mule's back. Later, this gun was superseded by an identical piece weighing 200 lbs with a barrel 3 ft 2 in. long. Iron cradles were used to carry the gun with its muzzle to the rear and the carriage-breast to the front while that cradle carrying the wheels had a special fitting.

In 1880 the famous 'screw-gun' (immortalized by Kipling) was introduced. This steel, rifled, muzzle-loading, jointed 7 pdr gun weighing 400 lbs was devised by Colonel C. B. le Mesurier RA, who increased the length and weight of the weapon by making the muzzle and breech in two portions, screwed together by a 'trunnion hoop'. This little gun threw its 7 lb projectile to great effect in many campaigns, and the mules could carry it by mountain paths and passes that caused the ordinary 9 pdr field guns to be left in the rear. It was usefully employed by Roberts in Afghanistan soon after its inception. However, in the 3rd Afghan War at Charasiah the mountain guns were of little use because of the high angle of elevation required to fire on an enemy up in the hills.

The mountain battery RA served with the Gordon Relief Column in 1884, carrying their 7 pdr steel screw-gun on camels. The two parts of the gun itself each made a load, the carriage and wheels made three more loads with three ammunition camels to each subdivision of one gun. The pack saddles weighed 120 lbs complete, the gun and carriage loads from 200–226 lbs and the

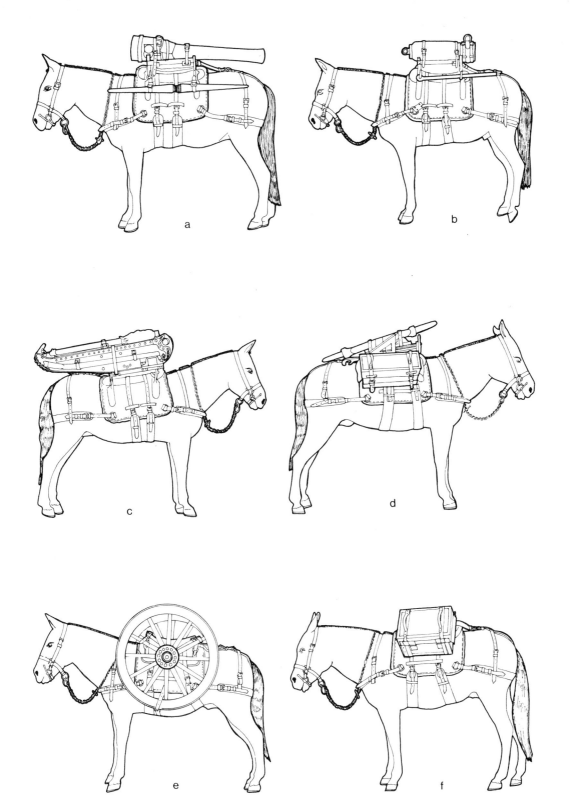

Fig. 78. First-line mules of a mountain battery, c. 1882, armed with the Armstrong 7-pdr screw-jointed steel gun. (a) *Muzzle;* (b) *Breech;* (c) *Carriage;* (d) *Axle, coupling block, trunnion guard, elevating gear, and two storage boxes;* (e) *Wheels;* (f) *ammunition.*

ammunition loads 220 lbs each. The officers, and an Egyptian officer and interpreter, the N.C.O.s and trumpeters were on riding camels; the gunners were mounted on baggage camels.

A highlight of the mountain gunners' history was their march with Colonel Kelly to relieve Chitral in 1895. Laboriously ploughing through deep, soft snow with the two guns slung on poles, everyone including the British officers took their turn at carrying. It was exhausting work as the gun and carriage loads each weighed 200 lbs and every ammunition box 125 lbs. So heavy were the loads that the carriers found it difficult to stay on the rough narrow beaten track; every few yards someone would tumble over causing load and bearers to be precipitated into the soft snow. The pace got slower and slower, finally the guns and loads were collected together and left behind, stacked in the snow and marked with upright poles. Considering it dangerous to leave a small number of men behind to guard the guns, the force marched on to the next camp for food and rest but on reaching the camp found that four men were missing. A non-commissioned officer and three gunners had stayed with their precious guns lest the enemy should arrive by night and capture them. In the late afternoon of the following day, exhausted and suffering snow-blindness, the gunners with their heavy loads staggered into camp. Delighted to see the two little guns, the force turned out to spontaneously cheer them in.

It had only been possible to manhandle four common and ten shrapnel shells per gun. Later when in action, as every shell had to count, it was necessary to get to very close range (about 400 yards) and, as the shells had no percussion fuses one of the precious common-shells had to be expended to ascertain the exact range. Under rifle fire, the gunners behaved with the utmost steadiness, exactly as if on parade as an officer ordered the shell to be fired and put up his glasses to observe it fall. Hearing no loud report, he lowered his glasses and turned to see all the gunners salaaming to the gun and to the shell, bidding 'God-speed' to the first round! In spite of their reverence, the shell fell short; the next round struck the foot of the sangar and the third caught it fair in the middle, knocking a big hole through it and scattering the men behind it. A few more rounds were fired until the combined infantry and artillery fire caused the enemy to retreat from his sangars. Then Colonel Kelly requested the artillery to silence a sangar which was at least 900 yards away. With only two or three common-shell left, the guns limbered up and advanced straight down the open slope towards the sangar until they arrived within 400 yards and under heavy fire came into action. The foresight of one gun was carried away by a bullet and the officer laid it by placing three fingers over the breech and sighting over them. The first shot blew a big hole through the sangar and the natives behind it ceased firing. At one period, there were so many men suffering from snow-blindness that not a gunner could see well enough to lay the guns.

Both officers and men of the mountain batteries seemed to be blessed with hawk-like vision that enabled them to pick out the lone Afridi sniper on the distant hillside who was holding up the advance with his stolen rifle. Few records of British Colonial small wars are without their accounts of the justly renowned British and Indian mountain batteries whose officers claimed that they could take their guns anywhere a man could go. They brought the use of mule transport to the point of perfection, displaying more tolerance than the Horse Artillery officer who said 'How we could gallop if it wasn't for those damn guns!'

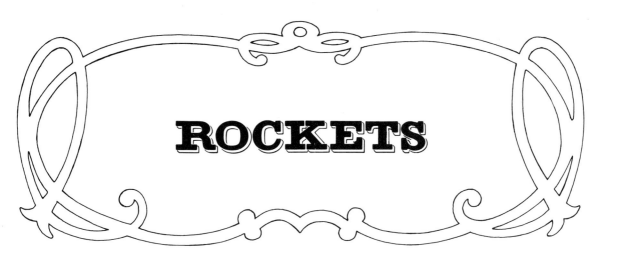

ROCKETS

As indicated by their revival in World War II, rockets have always been attractive weapons because they are cheap, their launching apparatus is simple and light, and large numbers of them can be fired in frightening salvoes. They were used in warfare by the Chinese before gunpowder was commonly employed and later by Indian princes – although these primitive projectiles displayed highly erratic tendencies.

In the early days of the nineteenth century the effective use at Copenhagen and Boulogne of rockets developed by Sir William Congreve led to the raising of a Rocket Brigade of the Royal Horse Artillery which saw action at Leipzig in 1813 and at Waterloo in 1815. In India the famous Bengal Horse Artillery formed a rocket troop in 1816 under the command of Captain Whish, its establishment was four British officers; ten European N.C.O.s; eighty European troopers; five Native officers; sixty Native camel drivers (sarwans) with seventy camels and twenty-six horses. Its armaments consisted of 960 12 lb. rockets, carried partly in four 'volley cars' and partly in buckets fixed to the camels' saddles.

Captain Whish's rocket troop were first used in February/March 1817, at the siege of Hattras when the fire of mortars and rockets caused the enemy to evacuate the city after only two days of bombardment. The rocket troop fired 138 rockets on the first day and it was recorded that although very unreliable, the rockets displayed a partial effect against their target and about 25 per cent. of them caused great terror by the wildness of their flight. Fired at 800 yards range, these 32 lb. rockets caused fires in the houses of the town; many landed in the fort some 800 yards beyond, but more than half missed both town and fort.

It is probable that, more than in any other campaign involving British or Indian artilleries, the first Burma War 1824–25 saw the most extensive use of rockets, as the Bengal Rocket Troop fired many flaming salvoes which ricochetted off the wooden stockades and obstacles, one killing the Burmese commander at a heavily defended position at Donabyo. Here, after a spirited start, the rockets' contribution to the second-half of the fire-plan was so poor as to arouse official enquiries which proved that the rockets behaving correctly were those which had travelled uneventfully by water; those giving an erratic or ineffective performance were those that had been shaken up by a rough road journey.

On 19 January 1826, during the attack on a strongly defended position at Melloon, of 304 rockets fired by the Rocket Troop only five failed to hit the target. Captain E. Buckle, a historian of the Bengal Artillery, wrote of this:

'The rocket practice was particularly efficient, scarce a rocket failed; in a strong contrast to the rockets carried by land, which had been proved worthless on several occasions; those used at Melloon were brought up by the flotilla, and perhaps never had there been an occasion since the invention of the weapon where they were more successful, their efforts could be so distinctly seen, as when, blazing and roaring, their long trails of smoke marking their course, they plunged into the stockades at Melloon and raked them from side-to-side in their eccentric courses after grazing.'

Throughout their history, when rockets have functioned correctly they have been most effective, particularly against high vertical surfaces such as walls and stockades, although there was always a marked inconsistency in their elevation and course. They seemed to be highly suitable for use from ships or boats where their simple and light launching gear could be utilized on a crowded deck and where the rockets themselves were not shaken by rough road journeys in unsprung vehicles.

As constituted at the outbreak of the Crimean War in 1854, Royal Artillery batteries carried 100 Congreve rockets in rocket waggons, and each mounted gunner carried two rockets. They were usually fired from tubes or pipes made of stout hard leather; they could be fired from the ground either singly or in volleys, especially against cavalry. The Royal Artillery rockets were 6 and 12 pdrs; against troops they had effective limits of about 600/1,000 yards according to their weight. Their cast hollow heads allowed bursting charges and a fuse to be inserted, so that they could be used as shell at short range. At Balaclava, Lt P. Dickson with the right division of 'W' battery, limbered up his guns on the approach of Russians and tried to continue to fire with rockets but a roundshot killed one of the wheel horses of the rocket waggon which narrowly escaped capture. At Inkerman some 24 pdr rockets were successfully fired by No. 1 Company of the 12th Battalion under Lt C. H. Owen; during the same battle, rockets were fired from the Victoria Ridge by sailors and by gunners from the 21 gun battery – seven 24 pdr rockets were fired from the right flank of 21 gun battery, to good effect, blowing up an ammunition waggon. At the Alma, 'E' battery fired a number of rockets, one killing eight men as it hissed through a Russian column.

Assiduously purchasing every available weapon from all quarters, it was perhaps inevitable that, during the American Civil War, the Confederacy should acquire rockets. They did not create much of an impression according to the report of Colonel W. W. Blackford CSA:

'Stuart opened on them with a Congreve rocket battery, the first and last time the latter ever appeared in action with us. It had been gotten up by some foreign chap who managed it on this occasion. They were huge rockets, fired from a sort of a gun carriage, with a shell at the end which exploded in due time, scattering 'liquid damnation', as the men called it. Their course was erratic; they went straight enough in their first flight, but after striking, the flight might be continued in any other course, even directly back towards where it came from. Great consternation was occasioned among the camps of the enemy as these unearthly serpents went zigzagging about among them. . . . A few tents were fired but the rockets proved to be of little practical value. . . .'

In the second half of the nineteenth century, the Hale rocket was a valiant attempt to stabilize this eccentric weapon by rotation of three metal vanes inserted in the exhaust nozzle; the Congreve was stabilized by a long stick. Chiefly valued for their psychological effect on unsophisticated opponents, Hale's rockets were exasperating weapons, notoriously inaccurate and incapable of hitting anything but large solid bodies at short ranges, their flight was erratic to the point of frequently endangering their crews. The propellant was a slow-burning mixture of nitre, charcoal and sulphur, forced into the case under great pressure; irregular burning or explosions were sometimes caused by fissuring of the packed propellant. The case of the rocket itself was of light iron; the warheads were solid and contained either explosive or incendiary materials. They were painted red with the mark, number and date of manufacture in black.

The 9 pdr rocket was $16\frac{1}{4}$ inches long and its cylinder was $2\frac{1}{2}$ inches in diameter; the 24

Fig. 79. 'The Rocket Troop', 1835. O Troop R.H.A. at exercise. (Coloured lithograph after William Heath.)

Fig. 80. 'Rocket Practice in the Marshes', 1845. (Coloured lithograph after J. Grant.)

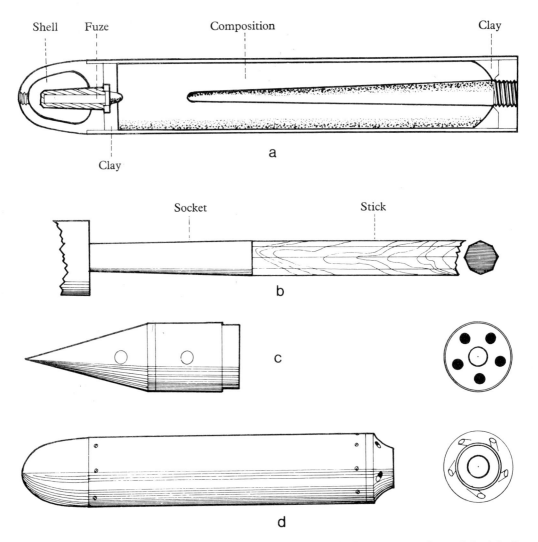

Shell   Fuze   Composition   Clay

Clay

a

Socket   Stick

b

c

d

Fig. 81. Rocket projectiles, c. 1860. (a) Congreve rocket; (b) Congreve rocket stick; (c) Carcass rocket head and base; (d) Hale's rocket and base.

pdr was 23 inches long and its diameter 4 inches. Ranges were:

At   5° elevation – 500/600 yards.
At 15° elevation – over 1,500 yards with an average deviation of 40 yards.

Fired by hand-lit fuses, the burning-time of the 9 pdr was roughly 8 seconds, the 24 pdr 10 seconds. In flight, rockets made a hideous shrieking noise, their passage being marked by a thick trail of white smoke dotted with yellow sparks.

In June 1868, a 'trough machine' was approved to launch the 9 pdr, and a month later for the 24 pdr. The 9 pdr launcher

weighed 27 lbs; the trough was 3 ft 5 in. long and the sides were 2½ in. wide; the 24 pdr launcher was 64¾ lbs, 5 ft 6 in. and 4 in. The launchers were painted black. Each was of the same basic pattern – a sheet-iron V-shaped trough, the sides of the trough meeting at an angle of 80 deg. The trough was supported at the rear by three legs of wrought-iron tubing, each ending in a prong; two short legs opened to left and right and a longer one to the front under the trough. A gun-metal ring ran along the front leg and was connected to the trough by two bars; elevation was obtained by sliding the ring up and down the front legs and clamping it on to the rear edge of the ring at the

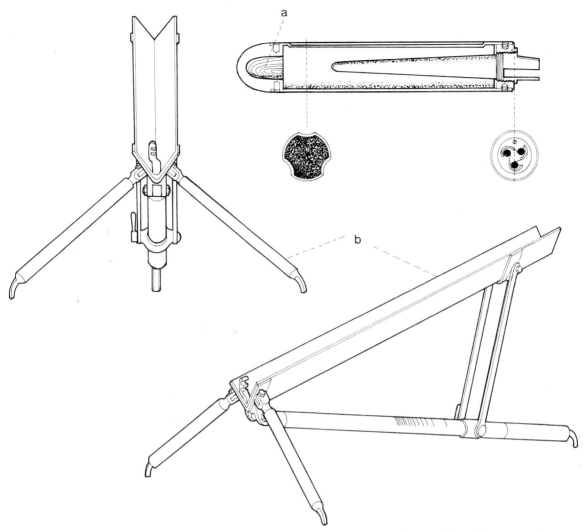

Fig. 82. Hale's rocket equipment, c. 1879. (a) *Rocket;* (b) *Two views of the firing trough.*

required line of graduation (up to 15 deg. for the 9 pdr and 25 deg. for the 24 pdr). There was an iron stop at the end of the trough to prevent the rocket sliding back and it was slotted to form a crutch for the copper friction tube.

Often manned by sailors of the Naval landing parties, rockets were used in the following Victorian campaigns:

Japan 1864.

Abyssinia 1868, when they were carried on mules.

Ashanti 1874.

Perak 1875/6.

Kaffir War 1877.

Zulu War 1879 – at Isandhlwana, where the Rocket Battery was formed of a bombar-dier and eight soldiers detailed from the 24th Regiment under Major Russell of the Royal Artillery, who rode a horse, while the men were mounted on the spare pack-mules that carried the battery.

Relief of Eshowe.

Ulundi.

1st Boer War 1881, where the Naval Brigade had a battery of rocket tubes, copper troughs set up on flimsy tripods (called by the Boers 'Cowhorns'). The rockets fired from these troughs were given directional guidance over a range of about a mile.

Benin 1897.

Niger 1897.

Egypt, at the Atbara 1898.

Fig. 83. The Rocket Brigade firing rockets at Senape during the Abyssinian expedition, 1868. (From the Illustrated London News.)

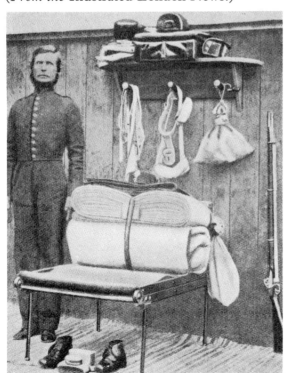

Fig. 84. A private of the Royal Fusiliers standing by his kit layout, c. 1864.

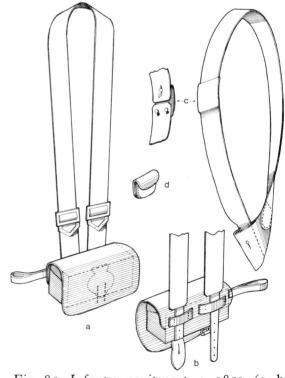

Fig. 85. Infantry equipment, c. 1850. (a, b) Foot Guards pattern cartouche box and belt; (c) Bayonet belt and plate; (d) Cap-pouch.

EQUIPMENT

Until recently, every infantryman had to march laden about his person with sufficient kit for his operational needs, and carry a firearm and bayonet, with an adequate and readily accessible supply of ammunition. Because the operationally essential amount of kit was sufficiently heavy to affect the soldier's fighting capabilities, a compromise was constantly sought between what was considered essential and what was physiologically sound.

The vertical frame of the human body is ill-adapted for the carriage of heavy loads by men in military formation marching in-step. From a strictly medical viewpoint a man should not carry more than 33 per cent. of his own weight (a horse, mule or camel not more than 25 per cent. of their weight) so the weight of the soldier's load should ideally be about 45 lbs, although industrial research indicates that a workman can carry a maximum weight of 88 lbs. Usually the soldier's load consisted of his fighting kit less his pack, or his marching load including the pack; either a greatcoat or a blanket weighing about 8 lbs, a water bottle (about 2 lbs) and probably 2 lbs of rations. Included in the kit itself were the so-called 'necessaries' – cleaning materials, spare boots, shirt and socks, usually carried in a haversack hanging on the left side below the belt. All this weighed about 30 lbs or so. The clothes, boots, etc., worn by the man totalled about another 12 lbs, making 40 lbs or more. Then there was the essential infantry shoulder musket or rifle weighing 18 lbs, plus $\frac{3}{4}$ lbs for some form of entrenching tool or axe. Climate and local conditions influenced a man's kit so that if both blanket and greatcoat were necessary in a cold climate, only one was carried in a more temperate area – only the blanket was borne during the Waterloo campaign.

Field-Marshal Sir John Burgoyne, who served in the Peninsula and in the Crimea, wrote: 'The British infantryman carried a load of arms and accoutrements considered by the peasantry under their ordinary habits to be impracticable.' Carrying 'enough for a donkey', Wellington's infantry were borne down by a load of 75 lbs (80 lbs if extra rations were carried). Rifleman Harris wrote that he was '. . . convinced that many of our infantry sank and died under the weight of their knapsacks alone . . . except the beef and biscuit, the eighty rounds of ball cartridges was the best thing he carried.' Riflemen carried twenty rounds more than the allowance for a Line regiment. Even in the ranks of such a professional and hard-fighting army as that led by Wellington in the Peninsula there were men who showed an unintelligent attitude towards their weapons and some British infantry of the period threw away their ammunition or sold it for drink; on one occasion Wellington noted that men ran out of cartridges after only five minutes of firing.

In the eighteenth century the soldier, after a toilet said to occupy three hours a day,

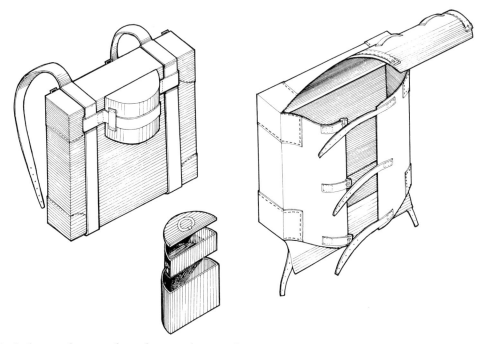

Fig. 86. Infantry knapsack and mess-tin, c. 1854.

looked very smart but was extremely uncomfortable. His hair needed curl papers and was tightly drawn back in a queue; his shako had to be balanced on his head which, for more than 50 years, was kept erect by a stock around his neck; cross belts compressed his chest and threw the sword back against the calves and the cartridge belt and haversack bumped against each other. Not until 1812 were his legs freed from long gaiters which impeded the circulation. From 1800 the soldier had to carry either a greatcoat in a linen bag on top of the knapsack or a blanket; until the mid-1860s he wore a knapsack squarely on the back with connected straps round each armpit.

During the Napoleonic Wars, British infantry wore belts across the chest and carried a cartridge box behind the right hip and a bayonet behind the left; Light infantry had a narrow waist belt to steady the cartridge box. In his book *Wellington's Army* Oman wrote that the load weighed between 50 and 60 lbs, varying with the amount of rations issued – the more rations carried by a soldier the more independent he was of transport; however it was considered unwise to trust the British soldier with more than one day's rations at a time, as he would im-

mediately eat as much as he could and either throw the rest away or give it to the local inhabitants, probably in return for drink or other favours.

In 1805 'Mr Trotter's knapsack' was issued, the forerunner of the various boxed-contraptions used for most of the century, with a wooden framework covered by a rectangular shape of painted canvas and supported by two arm-pit straps with another connecting them across the chest. A lighter knapsack was issued in 1824, constructed to fit closely to the back, it attempted to relieve the loins; no attempts was made to balance the load by carrying some part of the soldier's kit in front. In 1829 the frame of the knapsack was strengthened, and in 1859 a smaller pattern was adopted, but it was not until 1871 that the 'box' was superseded.

In the mid-eighteenth century, the cartridge-box hung inconveniently and the soldier found it so difficult to extract his cartridges that he had to ask his right-hand man to take out the bottom layer. To avoid this he extracted several rounds at a time and tucked them into the waist band of the breeches, a practice that was continued well into the nineteenth century, causing cartridges to fall out and be lost. In the 1840s a new waist belt

Fig. 87. Above: *Infantry equipment, 1854.* Left: *Foot Guards with shoulder bayonet belt.* Right: *Highlanders with waist bayonet belt. Note that the personal kit was carried wrapped in a blanket instead of in a knapsack.* Below: *Cavalry equipment, 1854.* Left: *Light dragoon.* Right: *Heavy dragoon.*

was issued, with a fob for the bayonet and a smaller pouch which could be refilled from the old cartridge-box on the cross-belt. The soldier carried his percussion caps in a small pouch either low down in a slit in the coatee on the right side or on the waist belt.

The cross-belt and cartridge-box, besides bumping the man's rear, were also tight over his chest, and the knapsack straps cut into the shoulders causing swelling, loss of strength and numbness of the hands and arms that lasted for perhaps 24 hours after a march. General Sir William Butler writing in 1866, describes how wearing the knapsack for 24 hours periods when on guard 'broke many a man's health down before he was forty'. He noted that the bandsmen, who never did guard duty, did not suffer in this way. Old soldiers called the condition 'them pains' and blamed the wearing of 'them belts'.

Private Robert Waterfield of the 32nd Regiment, who chronicled his Army life in the 1840s, was inspired by such discomforts to write: '. . . what with hard duties and bad rations, I began to tire of the honourable profession of arms. I was rather slight, and the knapsack caused great pain in my chest, but I was growing very fast at this time and a civilian doctor, who attended the sick of my company, told me I should outgrow the disease.' Later Waterfield was unable to wear his knapsack because of the difficulty of breathing and in May 1843 he was invalided and sent to Chatham with twenty-nine other invalids. After six weeks in hospital and some weeks inactivity, he was ordered to go to the garrison barracks and try a month's duty but after putting the knapsack on once he found it hurt as much as ever. Waterfield wrote: 'Nevertheless I was determined to sink under it rather than complain again. I was brought up again and again examined by several doctors. I told them I was free from pain even when I had the pack on, which was false. I remember that one doctor almost put the words into my mouth to say that the "pack still hurt me" but I knew that all the blistering and cupping in the world would not benefit me any, for my left breast was much larger than the right one; as I grew I noticed that my left breast gradually dimin-

ished in size, and I often thought that when I ceased to grow I would be alright again.'

With a few minor variations, the equipment of the British soldier remained virtually unchanged from 1790 until 1850 so that he was accoutred in the Crimea much as at Waterloo. The troops who struggled ashore at Calamita Bay in the Crimea on Thursday 14 September 1854, wore full dress, carried slung over one shoulder a wooden canteen of water and over the other a haversack containing rations for three days – $4\frac{1}{2}$ lbs of cooked salt meat and a bulky package of the same amount of biscuit. Each man carried a part of the mess cooking apparatus, a musket and bayonet, a cartridge-box and fifty rounds of ball cartridge. Before landing, the medical authorities (to lessen the burden carried by the sick soldiers) recommended that knapsacks be left on board ship. The blanket was to carry the man's necessary 'small' kit – towel, soap, razor, spare boots, two spare neck-stocks, two shirts, two pairs socks, boot blacking and brushes, and a forage-cap (taken at the men's special request to replace the top-heavy and uncomfortable shako). Later it was claimed that much of the soldier's subsequent suffering could be attributed to this well-intentioned but ignorant alteration to his equipment with all its accompanying inconvenience and loss, as the knapsacks were all ransacked on the ships. To form a roll or pack out of a heavy blanket, with greatcoat and mess tin on top was no easy achievement and on the line of march it soon caused great discomfort by sinking heavily from the shoulders to the small of the back.

At this time, in full marching order, the standard equipment of the soldier consisted of two crossbelts, one holding the ammunition and pouch and the other the bayonet in a fob, fastened on the chest with a regimental-pattern crossbelt plate. Carried on the back, the large pack (or knapsack) was made of blackened canvas reinforced with wooden slats and bound along the bottom and corners with leather; the regimental badge or number was painted in its centre. The pack was supported by two white straps passing round the arms at the shoulders and kept in position by another strap across the chest.

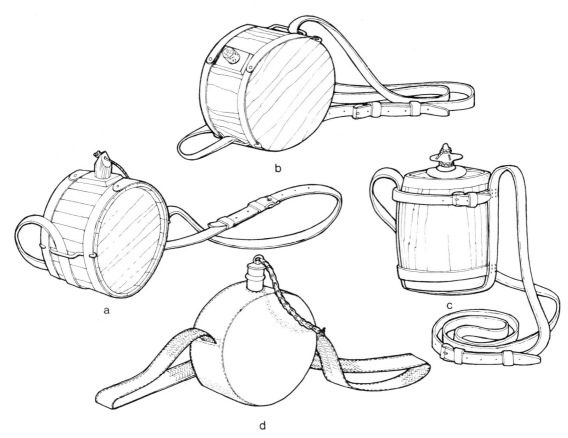

Fig. 88. (a) *Wooden water canteen, c. 1850;* (b) *Wooden canteen, c. 1865;* (c) *'Oliver' pattern water-bottle, c. 1870;* (d) *Metal water-bottle in linen cover, c. 1900.*

On top of the pack was the D-shaped mess tin in its black oil skin cover and the tightly-rolled greatcoat or blanket. There was quite an art in rolling a top-coat, two or three men assisted in the actual rolling, but the art lay in arranging the coat on the floor or table beforehand. A white canvas haversack was carried on the left-hand side and a round wooden waterbottle on the right.

The bayonet fob belt and the crossbelt fastened by the ornamental belt plate was replaced in 1850 with a single waist belt with a brass locket but delay in issuing new kit meant that many soldiers did not get it until 1854–5.

When a man was carrying three day's rations and a blanket his load totalled about 68 lbs but, during the Kaffir campaign in 1852, the 73rd were laden with two blankets, a greatcoat, seventy rounds and seven day's rations. By order of Major-General Sir William Eyre 'a fine fighting soldier with a violent temper' on marches that were long and extremely arduous, stragglers were punished by having their blankets and rations burned. In 1854, encamped next to Zouaves at Gallipoli, the Rifle Brigade discovered that the Frenchmen easily carried far more weight than that which caused riflemen to straggle and fall-out of the line-of-march. George Higginson of the Grenadier Guards wrote:

'. . . I intend as quietly as I can to abolish stocks, etc., to see if we cannot make a good start when we do take the field.'

Mostly the Victorian soldier was involved in campaigns against natives burdened with little else but their weapons and perhaps a shield. These operations often involved hand-to-hand fighting and the soldier, probably physically inferior and less hardy than his native opponent, was greatly handicapped by the encumbrances of kit and equipment. Occasionally this was realized

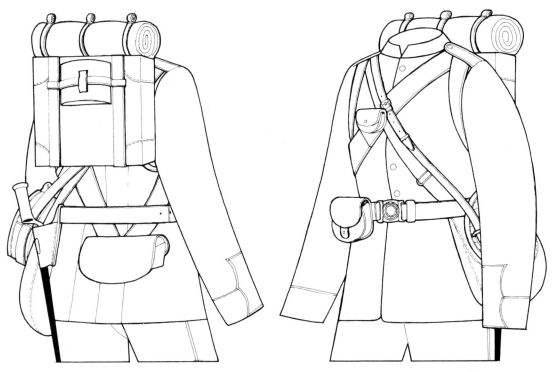

Fig. 89. Infantry equipment, c. 1860. This is the equipment shown in the kit layout in Fig. 84.

when 'operational essentials' were carried on pack animals or wheeled transport. In 1888, during the operations of the Hazara Field Force on the North-West Frontier of India, the officers were allowed half a mule load of baggage while the infantry were permitted only 16 lbs of kit. No tents were taken and each man had seventy rounds of ammunition – thirty rounds per rifle were loaded on to the mules and five days' supplies were carried. On the advance to the Atbara in April 1898, four lightly-equipped brigades of infantry marched into the desert in column of brigade squares. The heavy baggage was left behind to its fate, the officers started with 30 lbs and the men with 9 lbs of kit. After a month and a half of General Gatacre, five miles with rifle and ammunition and 9 lbs of kit might not seem excessive to the British soldier, but in a country where the thermometer invariably exceeded a hundred degrees in the shade it meant a lot of hardship.

In 1855, the general-issue equipment consisted of a white crossbelt holding a slightly smaller ammunition pouch and a small white buff pouch for percussion caps. The waist

belt had a bayonet frog and, for active service, another black leather ammunition pouch was fitted to its right front. The remainder of the equipment was as previously worn. In 1856 the knapsack was reduced in size and the chest-connecting strap discontinued. In 1860 a new pattern white leather pouch was issued, to be worn on the waist belt in place of the black one.

In 1869 in his '*Soldiers' Pocketbook*', Lord Wolseley came out strongly against the knapsack (which he called a pack as did most of the soldiers) '... it is absurd to expect a man to carry a portmanteau full of things on his back.' He opposed spare boots, shirt, etc., being included in the soldier's load and suggested that he carried a waterproof sheet with straps to hold a blanket, greatcoat, one shirt, one pair of socks, one towel and a piece of soap. This totalled 14 lbs and, by dispensing with the pack which weighed 3 lbs 3 ozs, Wolseley claimed that the total weight carried would be 43 lbs 2 ozs including the man's clothing and one day's rations – a considerable reduction from the 56 lbs 12½ ozs carried in heavy marching order. During the Zulu War of 1879, the men carried pouches

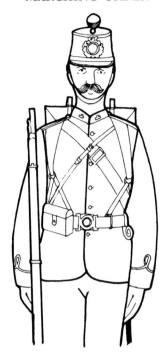

ORDINARY
MARCHING ORDER

SERVICE
MARCHING ORDER

Serge-coat, one Pouch, Water bottle,
Haversack, Greatcoat, forage-cap
on the Coat, Valise.

Serge-coat, two Pouches, Ammunition
bag, Haversack, Water bottle, Cape
under flap, Mess-tin, Greatcoat,
Forage cap between Coat straps.

Fig. 90. Infantry valise equipment, c. 1875. This is the equipment shown in the kit layout in Fig. 5.

and a haversack and slung everything else into a company waggon; fully accoutred, with rifle, seventy rounds of ammunition and two days' rations, each man carried 57 lbs.

In 1868 sets of a new pattern of equipment were issued on trial to selected N.C.O.s of the Royal Marines at Plymouth; considered successful, this valise equipment superseded knapsacks in the Royal Marines in January 1870, and in the 2nd Bn Rifle Brigade in February. Designed to evenly distribute weight by bearing most of it on the shoulder straps, the equipment consisted of a waist belt, divided cross-braces, a bayonet frog, two black leather pouches and a black valise with mess-tin, blanket, haversack and water-bottle. The Guards and the 29th Foot had white pouches instead of black. Fastened to the waist belt at the front, the cross-belts passed over the shoulders, crossed at the

back and fastened back to the braces at the front. Resting on the buttocks with the blanket rolled above, the valise was attached to brass rings at the front on the braces. A black leather pouch was carried on the belt at the front, hanging below the right pouch and, when the valise was not worn, the pouch was suspended from the intersection of the braces by a white buff strap.

Generally introduced into the Army in 1871, the valise equipment involved considerable changes such as the knapsack being replaced by a black waterproof canvas bag or valise worn at the small of the back and supported over the shoulders by straps split into three at the level of the third button of the tunic. These straps fastened to a waist belt holding two pouches, one on each side of the belt clasp, each containing twenty rounds with a further thirty rounds carried in a 'ball

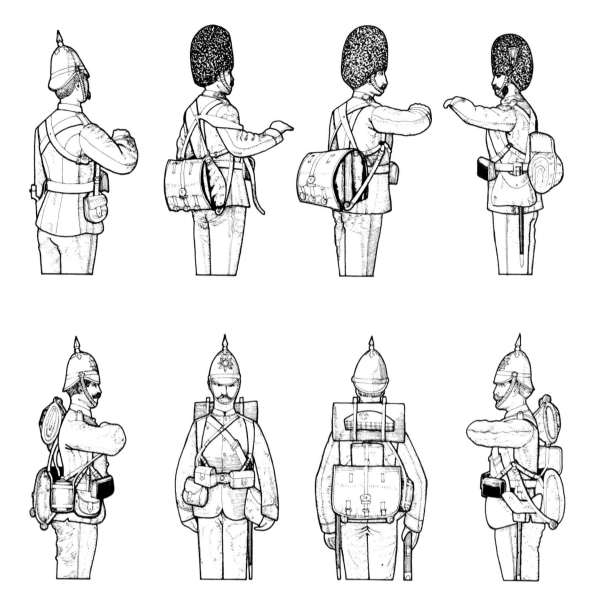

Fig. 91. *Different orders of dress and methods of fitting the valise equipment. (From illustrations issued with General Orders of 1 May 1885.)*

bag' slung below the right-hand pouch. When full, these pouches partially balanced the valise which had the rolled cape and the mess-tin level with the man's neck. The cross-belt with the old semi-inaccessible cartridge box disappeared. For the first and last time, the pack (or valise as it was now) was carried low, well below the shoulders. Longer than before, the bayonet was carried on the left side of the waist belt with the haversack in a position that caused it to catch between a man's legs when he doubled. In *Sea*

to Sea, Vol. I, Chapter XV, Kipling wrote: '. . . when doubling clutching at the bayonet to keep it from tripping them up, as one can see in running firing on ranges in India at any time.'

When firing in the prone position, ammunition tended to fall out of the pouches; this was a big handicap as the introduction of the rapid breech-loader meant that a considerable amount of firing was done in this position. When firing from behind low cover a soldier could be shot through the right

Fig. 92. Infantry equipment as worn during the Zulu War, 1879. Note that the valise was not worn.

elbow as he put up his arm to extract a round from his right-hand pouch. Hurriedly rising to his feet to advance at the double, the soldier had to fasten the pouch, grab at the bayonet to keep it clear of his legs and steady his head-dress to stop it falling off, besides carrying a rifle at the same time.

In his autobiography Sir William Butler reveals that in about 1878, an officer of the 60th Rifles invented a very complete and highly sensible set of military equipment of belts, knapsack and other accoutrements, very much lighter and easier to put on, take off or carry than the existing equipment. It was very much liked by soldiers who had tried out the new patterns both on guard and on the march, declaring them lighter, easier to manipulate and wear than the old heavy, stiff and hard equipment that had caused so much discomfort to infantry soldiers for so long. In spite of this the War Office repeatedly refused to take the new equipment into general use; Butler believed because of the behind-the-scenes influence wielded by the Army contractors who supplied the old-style equipment.

In 1882, a new pattern valise equipment was introduced which retained the pouches (now white) but with the valise worn high, its top level with the armpits; the rolled greatcoat was carried on the waist belt with the mess-tin above it. This pattern had the serious disadvantage of being difficult to change from heavy marching order with the valise to light marching order without it; the valise was stated 'not to ride well on the man for a long march' (RUSI *Journal* 1888, page 459). A new issue was an entrenching tool weighing 3 lbs consisting of a small pick and shovel with a single handle, carried with the bayonet on the waist belt. Strict orders were given that it was to be '. . . carefully preserved for employment in the presence of the enemy and not to be used for regular entrenchments or for camp fatigues.'

In 1888, Colonel Slade (Rifle Brigade) and Lt-Col. Wallace (King's Royal Rifle Corps) introduced their equipment, made of leather although webbing was already coming into use as a substitute in army equipment. Designed for any climate it came to be known as the 'Slade-Wallace' equipment and

Fig. 93. Field Service Equipment Pattern, 1882.

consisted of a waist belt and harness supporting two forty-round ammunition pouches; behind the shoulders supported by shoulder braces was a glazed-leather valise (bearing the regimental badge) containing field kit and twenty rounds of ammunition; below the valise hung the mess-tin and rolled greatcoat; crossbelts supported a water canteen on the right hip and a haversack on the left which, when not in use, was rolled into a pad; the bayonet scabbard was slung on the left side of the belt. In the field, the white Slade–Wallace harness, pouches and haversack were stained (sometimes with tea) to a neutral shade. A great advantage of this equipment was that the reduced-in-size valise could speedily be removed and replaced by the haversack, waterproof sheet or blanket. Riding high on the shoulders, the valise was fastened to two cross-braces with a strap held by a brass D on the shoulder and engaging the double brass buckle on the front of the brace, with the mess-tin in an oilskin cover and the rolled blanket attached

Fig. 94. Left: *An officer of the Grenadier Guards photographed before leaving for Egypt, 1882.*

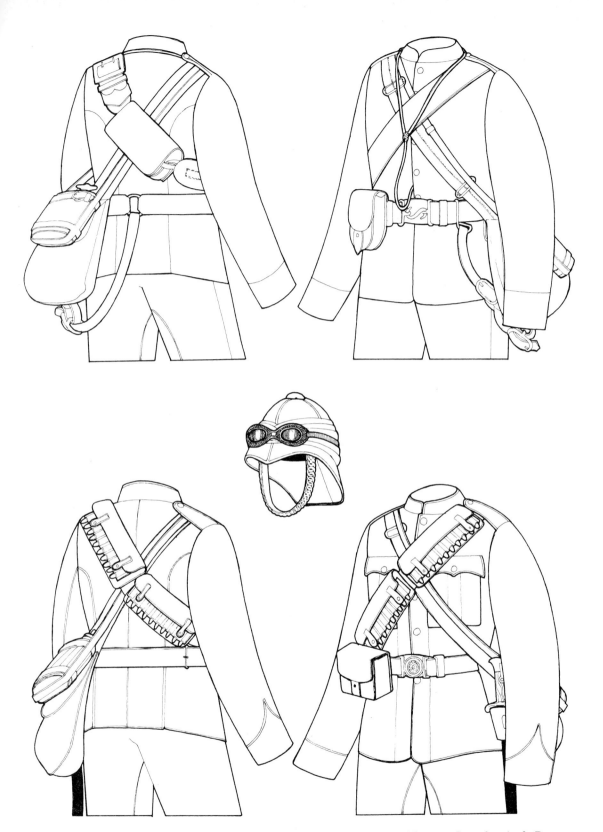

Fig. 95. Equipment worn during the 1st Sudan campaign, 1884. Above: Cavalry (4th Dragoon Guards). Below: Guards Camel Regiment.

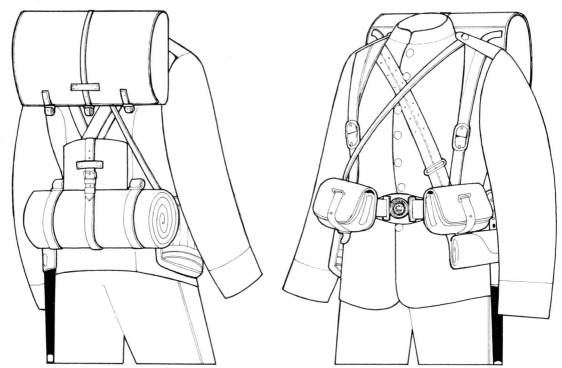

Fig. 96. Field Service Equipment Pattern, 1888. Known as the 'Slade-Wallace' equipment, parts of which, e.g., the waist-belt, are still in use.

to the belt below the valise. The waist belt carried two forty-round ammunition pouches and for a short time a ten-round magazine was worn on the left brace in a small pouch above the ammunition pouch.

In heavy marching order the complete weight was 41 lbs; including arms, ammunition and uniform, the man carried 56 lbs, reduced to 38 lbs when the valise was carried on regimental transport as was usually the case in India and Africa. The knapsack and the valise which superseded it in 1871, were never carried in India or Abyssinia in 1867; nor in any campaigns in South Africa, in Egypt in 1882–5 or in Burma. Dressed as privates with full heavy marching order kits, four officers stationed at Portsmouth carried out a route march to London. They covered 35 miles to Farnham on the first day and 24 miles to Wickham on the second day, being inspected at Aldershot en route, on the third day they marched 28 miles to London where they were inspected by Army H.Q. including Lord Wolseley. Considered to be successful, the trial revealed that if no ammunition was carried the waist belt would have to be considerably tightened to keep the weight on the back dragging it up.

At this time the weight of arms and accoutrements was 16 lbs 2 ozs with ammunition weighing 5 lbs 7 ozs, although more ammunition was being carried without an increase in weight because reductions in the calibre of rifle made the ammunition, round for round, lighter than before. These were the days of the newly-introduced Snider breech-loading rifle, taking a cartridge and using the percussion cap.

For the Martini–Henry .45 in. rifle, seventy rounds of ammunition were carried; ninety with the Lee–Metford magazine rifle of .303 inches, with ten more rounds added in 1888 and eighty rounds were carried with the Lee–Enfield of 1892. Ignoring the foreign practice of loading magazine-arms with clips or chargers usually holding five rounds, for a short time the British infantryman was issued with a second ten-round magazine carried on the left brace above the pouch. This meant that pouches were retained while the soldier continued to re-load with single rounds.

From 1878 onwards the British Army had been experimenting with webbing shoulder belts called bandoliers made to hold fifty/fifty-four rounds of Snider .577 and

Fig. 97. Typical equipment worn during the 2nd Sudan campaign, 1898. Above: *Infantry.* Below: *Cavalry (21st Lancers). Note the quilted cotton spine pads and neck covers for the helmet.*

123

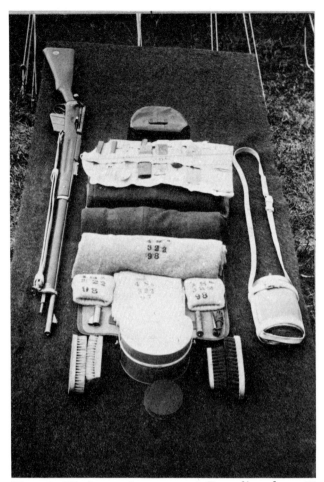

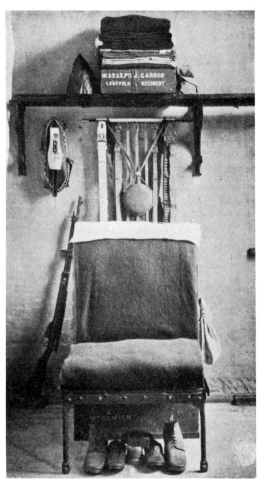

Fig. 98. Kit layout in camp. 4th Battalion the Suffolk Regiment, c. 1890.

Fig. 99. Kit layout in barracks. 1st Battalion the Suffolk Regiment, c. 1900. Published as a guide by the War Office.

Martini cartridges; each cartridge held in a loop with leather covers fastening over the loops to retain the rounds. Loading was easy from the bandoliers although in wet weather the cartridges sometimes had to be eased up from below with the finger. Fighting the Spaniards in the Philippines in 1898, United States infantry wore web waist belts that held 100 rounds of ammunition in two rows; they were not entirely satisfactory as the loops holding the ammunition stretched and the rounds fell out when men stooped or lay down. The British Government ordered a large number of these belts through William Lindsey of Boston, U.S.A., who subsequently set up a small plant in North London and manufactured them. This was the start in Great Britain of the Mills Equipment Company which has been responsible for the equipment of the British Army ever since.

When the South African War of 1899–1901 broke out, the British Infantry wore the Slade–Wallace equipment with two pouches on the front of the body and the mounted infantry wore a fifty-round bandolier. The commandos of the two Republics of the Transvaal and the Orange Free State wore fifty-round leather bandoliers with pockets each holding a five-round clip for their Mauser rifle. The British infantryman went to war less encumbered than ever before, carrying the rolled greatcoat on his waist belt at the back, with the mess-tin on top and without a valise; the whole weighing a little over 25 lbs.

To cope with the serious shortage of bandoliers, the mounted infantry were issued

Fig. 100. Sergeants of the 1st Battalion the Northumberland Fusiliers in Foreign Service Order, c. 1899. (Photograph by Stuart.)

with canvas carriers normally part of the equipment of the battalion ammunition mules, transporting cartridges to the firing line when it was impossible to carry a box from the mule. Disposable flimsy woven bandoliers, holding 100 rounds in loops, were issued. Quickly wearing out, they allowed thousands of rounds of ammunition to be lost in the field. This was turned to good account by the Boers who were running short of ammunition for their Mausers but had large numbers of captured Lee–Enfields. In his book *Commando*, Denys Reitz wrote:

'We were getting short of ammunition (as it was in 1901) so during the next two days we followed the road by which the English had travelled to pick up their cartridges. They were notoriously careless of their ammunition and if a round or two dropped from their bandoliers they would never trouble to dismount, as they knew they could get more, and at their halting places one could almost always find cartridges lying spilt in the grass. Latterly it became a regular practice to trail the columns, sometimes for a week on end, to glean these crumbs from a rich man's table, and I doubt if the British ever realized to what an extent the Boers were dependent on this sort of replenishment.'

Commenting on this serious loss of ammunition, Kitchener later attributed it mainly to '. . . the unsuitability of the articles supplied to the individual soldier in which to carry his rounds.'

Later in the war leather bandoliers, with flaps fastening over to hold their fifty rounds in place, were issued and worn over the shoulders or round the waist; mounted men often carried a second bandolier around the horse's neck.

Immediately after the South African War, the British Army rearmed with a new version of the Lee–Enfield rifle that used clips of five cartridges to replenish the ten-round magazine. In 1903, the bandolier equipment

Fig. 101. Infantry bandolier equipment as worn in the South African War. This equipment is shown in the kit layout in Fig. 99.

was issued; weighing about 40 lbs, it had the pack replaced by the folded greatcoat carried high; the mess-tin was below the coat on the waist belt, which was a bandolier with five pockets, each holding two clips of five rounds, with a second bandolier over the left shoulder holding a further fifty rounds.

In Paris in 1902, while the South African War was still in progress, Commandant E. Laviss of the French Army wrote a most authoritative book *Sac au Dos*, concerning the weight of kits carried by infantry of the major armies of Europe and of the United States. He revealed that the 28·5 kilos carried by American infantry was the highest weight of any army, but the highest load of any unit was the 32 kilos pack, etc., of the French Chasseurs Alpins. German soldiers carried 26·7 kilos; Russian soldiers 26·4

kilos; French soldiers 24·4 kilos (plus a section of tent that weighed an additional 2·6 kilos); British soldiers carried 23·6 kilos, with a mean weight of 26·5 kilos (about 58 lbs). Laviss believed that with about 60 lbs maximum load, the British soldier with Slade–Wallace equipment was slightly below his maximum. The author was very much against the German practice of carrying extra rounds in the pack or haversack because of the difficulty of getting to the pack during an action. Similarly, he was strongly against the pack being carried by transport and stated that he did not believe that the soldier should ever be separated from his pack. Such views were of interest in view of the fact that Britain was within measurable distance of fighting a major war on the Continent.

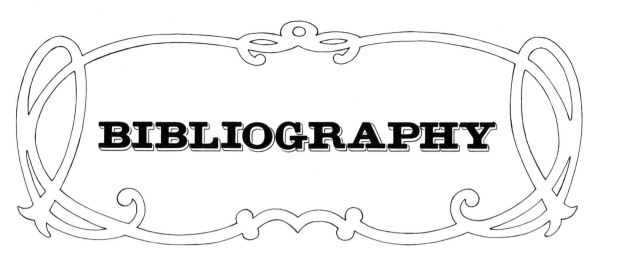

BIBLIOGRAPHY

Aylward, J. D., *The Small Sword in England* (1960).

Bailey, D. W., *British Military Longarms 1815–1865* (1972).
Batchelor, J. and Hogg, I., *Artillery* (1974).
Blackmore, H. L., *British Military Firearms* (1961).
——, *Firearms* (1964).
——, *Guns and Rifles of the World* (1965).

Chown, J. D., *The 9 pdr Muzzle Loading Rifle* (1967).
Coggins, Jack, *Arms and Equipment of the Civil War* (1962).

Downey, Fairfax, *The Guns at Gettysburg* (1958).
——, *Sound of the Guns* (1955).

Foulkes, C. J., *Sword, Lance and Bayonet* (1937).
Fuller, C. E., *The Rifled Musket* (1958).
Fuller, J. F. C., *Armament and History* (1945).

George, J. N., *English Pistols and Revolvers* (1938).
——, *English Guns and Rifles* (1947).
Graham, C. A. L., *The History of the Indian Mountain Artillery* (1957).
Griffiths, F. A., *The Artillerist's Manual and British Soldier's Compendium* (1839–59).

Headlam, Sir John, *History of the Royal Artillery 1860–1914* (n.d.).

Held, R., *The Age of Firearms* (1957).
Hilliard, A. and Longstaff, F. V., *The Book of the Machine Gun* (1917).
Hughes, B. P., *British Smoothbore Artillery* (1969).
——, *The Bengal Horse Artillery* (1971).
——, *Firepower* (1974).
Hutton, A., *Cold Steel* (1889).
——, *Fixed Bayonets* (1890).

Jocelyn, J. R. J., *The History of the Royal Artillery* (1911).

MacFetridge, C. H. and Warren, J. P., *Tales of the Mountain Gunners* (1973).
Muancy, A., *Artillery Through the Ages* (1956).
Moore, W., *Guns* (1963).
Moyse-Bartlett, H., *Louis Edward Nolan and His Influence on the British Cavalry* (1971).
Myatt, F., *The Soldier's Trade* (1974).

Naisawald, L. V. L., *Grape and Canister* (1960).

Peterson, H. L., *Encyclopaedia of Firearms* (1968).
——, *Roundshot and Rammers* (1974).
Pridham, C. H. B., *Superiority of Fire – a short history of rifles and machine guns* (1945).

Renbourn, E. T., *The Knapsack and Pack* (1952).
Reynolds, E. G. B., *The Lee-Enfield Rifle* (1960).

Ricketts, H., *Firearms* (1962).

Roads, C. H., *The British Soldier's Firearm 1850–64* (n.d.).

Rogers, H. B. C., *Weapons of the British Soldier* (1960).

Rowbotham, W., *The Naval Brigade in the Indian Mutiny* (1947).

Smith, J. E. and Smith, W. H. B., *Small Arms of the World* (1960).

Stephens, F., *Bayonets* (1968).

Stubbs, F. W., *History of the Bengal Artillery* (1895).

Toppel, D. and Wahl, P., *The Gatling Gun* (1966).

Verney, G. L., *The Devil's Wind* (1956).

Weller, Jac, *Weapons and Tactics* (1966).

Wilkinson, F., *Small Arms* (1965).

——, *Swords and Daggers* (1967).

——, *Guns* (1970).

——, *Edged Weapons* (1970).

Wilkinson-Latham, J., *Evolution of Swords* (1962).

——, *British Military Swords* (1960).

——, *Regulation Military Swords* (1970).

——, *British Cut and Thrust Weapons* (1971).

——, *British Army Equipment* (1972).

Wilson, A. W., *The Story of the Gun* (1944).

Young, Peter, *The Machinery of War* (1973).

Journal of Army Historical Research.

Journal of the Royal United Service Institution.

Cavalry Journal.

Illustrated London News.

Army and Navy Gazette.

United Service Gazette.

INDEX

Page numbers in italic refer to illustration pages. Entries beginning with numerals will be found at the end of the index.